PAUL SIMON

So Beautiful or So What

T0056658

Wise Publications
part of The Music Sales Group
London / New York / Paris / Sydney / Copenhagen /
Berlin / Madrid / Hong Kong / Tokyo

PUBLISHED BY
WISE PUBLICATIONS
14-15 BERNERS STREET, LONDON W1T 3LJ, UK.

EXCLUSIVE DISTRIBUTORS:
MUSIC SALES LIMITED
DISTRIBUTION CENTRE, NEWMARKET ROAD, BURY ST EDMUNDS,
SUFFOLK IP33 3YB, UK.
MUSIC SALES CORPORATION
257 PARK AVENUE SOUTH, NEW YORK, NY 10010, USA.
MUSIC SALES PTY LIMITED
20 RESOLUTION DRIVE, CARINGBAH, NSW 2229, AUSTRALIA.

ORDER NO. PS11715
ISBN: 978-1-78038-131-2

EDITED BY JENNI WHEELER.
MUSIC ARRANGED BY DEREK JONES.
MUSIC PROCESSED BY PAUL EWERS MUSIC DESIGN.
PRINTED IN THE EU.

Getting Ready for Christmas Day

Words & Music by Paul Simon

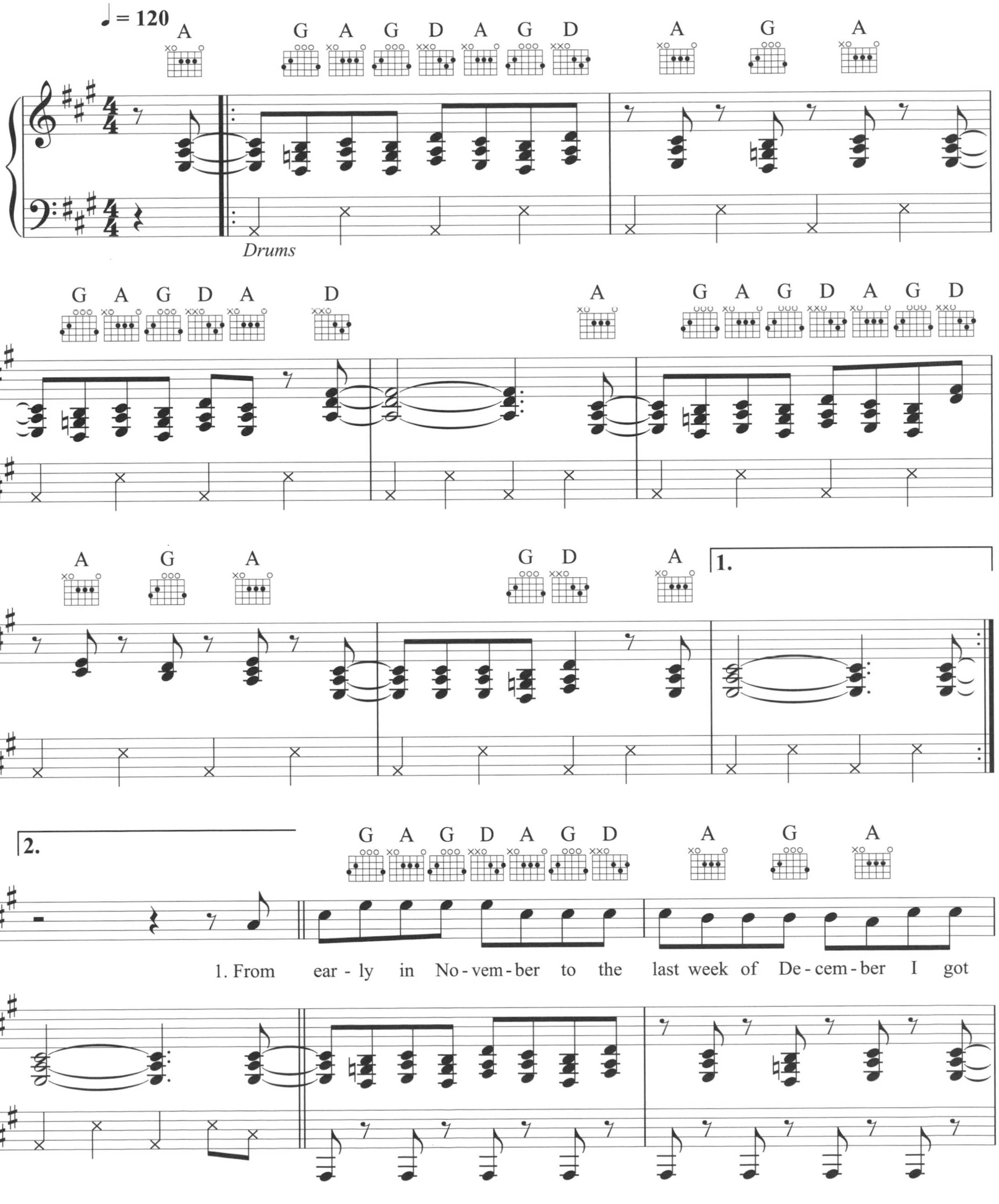

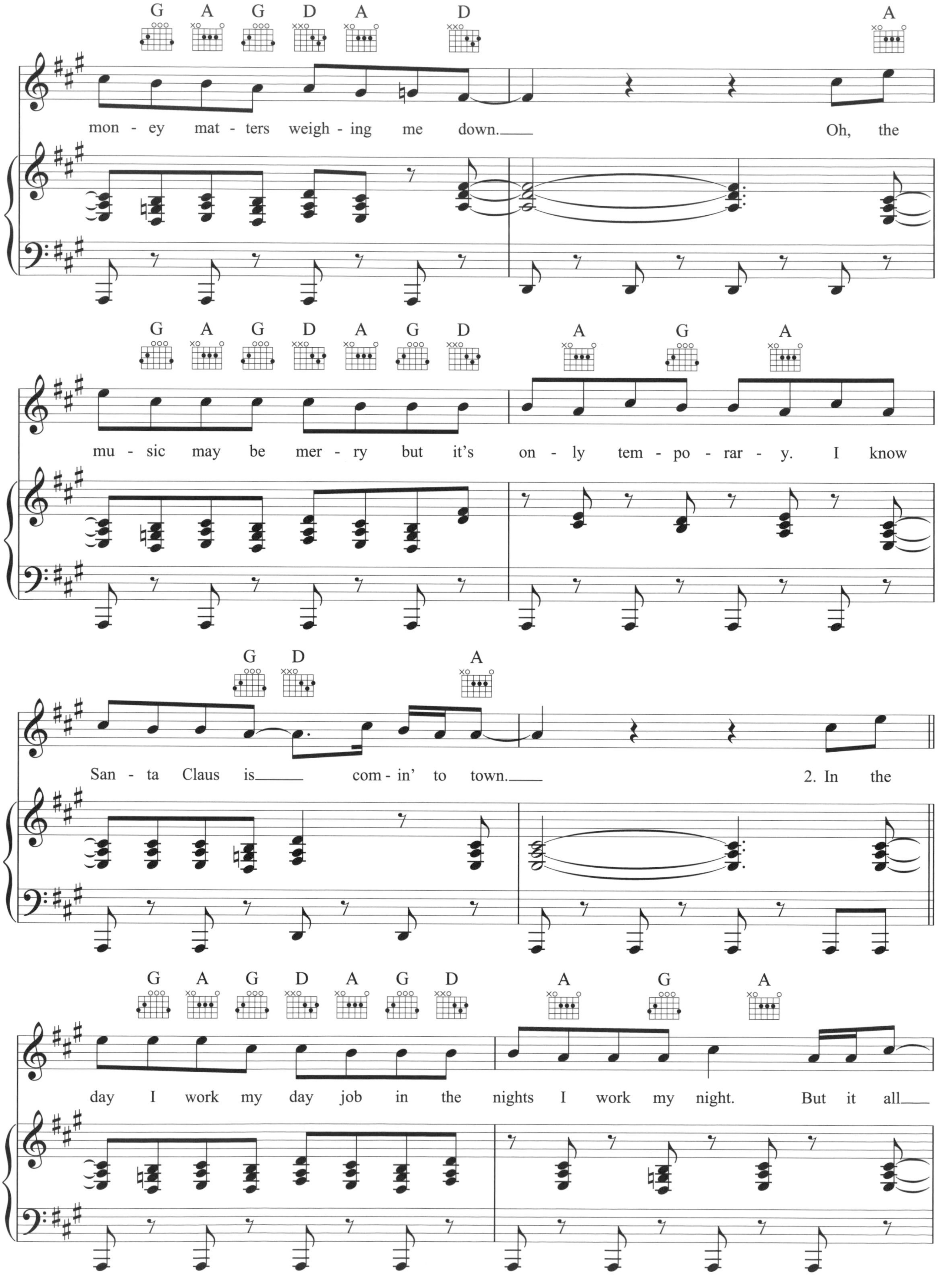
G A G D A D A
mon - ey mat - ters weigh - ing me down. Oh, the
G A G D A G D A G A
mu - sic may be mer - ry but it's on - ly tem - po - rar - y. I know
G D A
San - ta Claus is com - in' to town. 2. In the
G A G D A G D A G A
day I work my day job in the nights I work my night. But it all

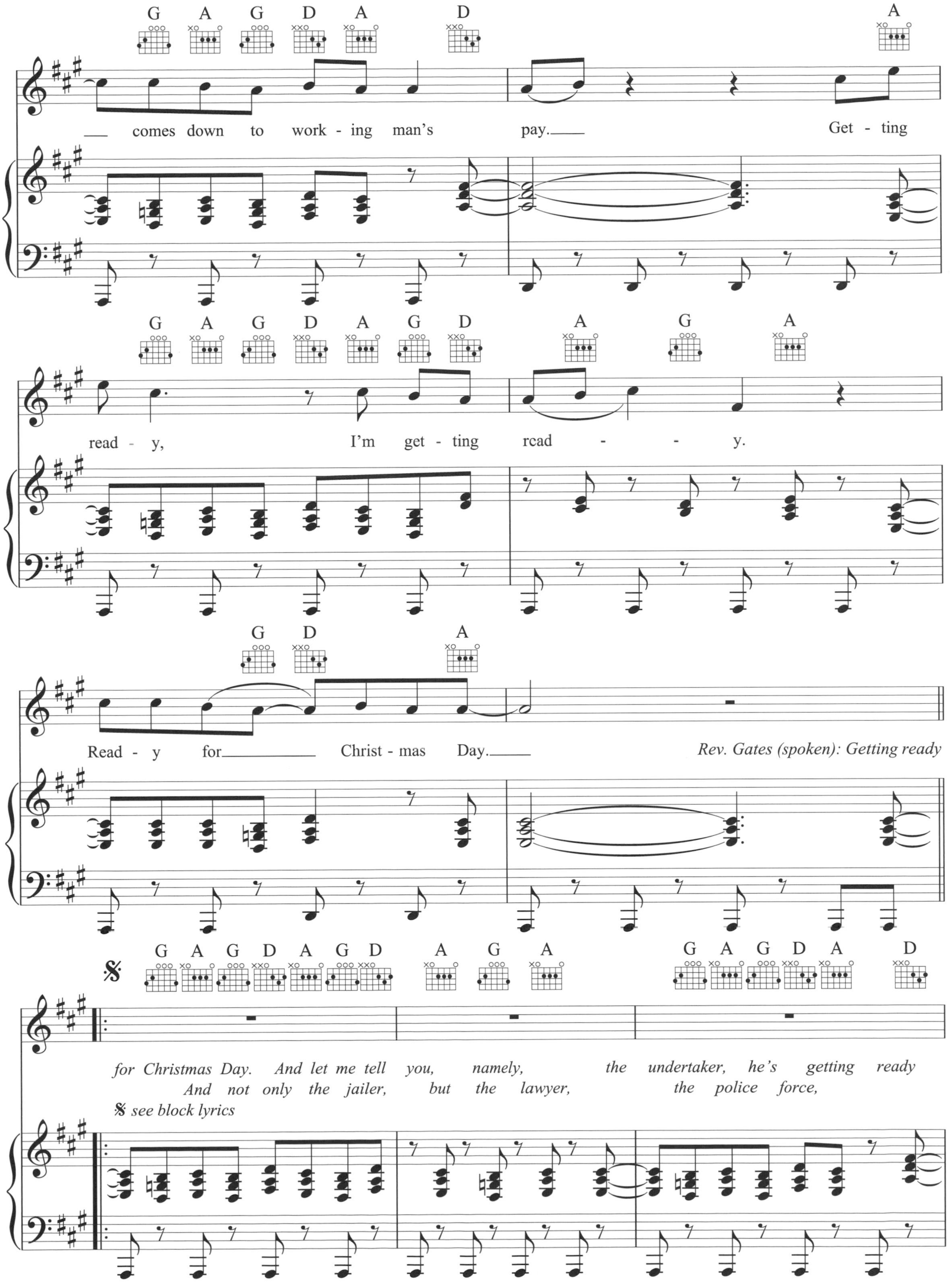
G A G D A D A
— comes down to work - ing man's pay.— Get - ting
G A G D A G D A G A
read - y, I'm get - ting read - - y.
G D A
Read - y for— Christ - mas Day.—
Rev. Gates (spoken): Getting ready
G A G D A G D A G A G A G D A D
for Christmas Day. And let me tell you, namely, the undertaker, he's getting ready
And not only the jailer, but the lawyer, the police force,
see block lyrics

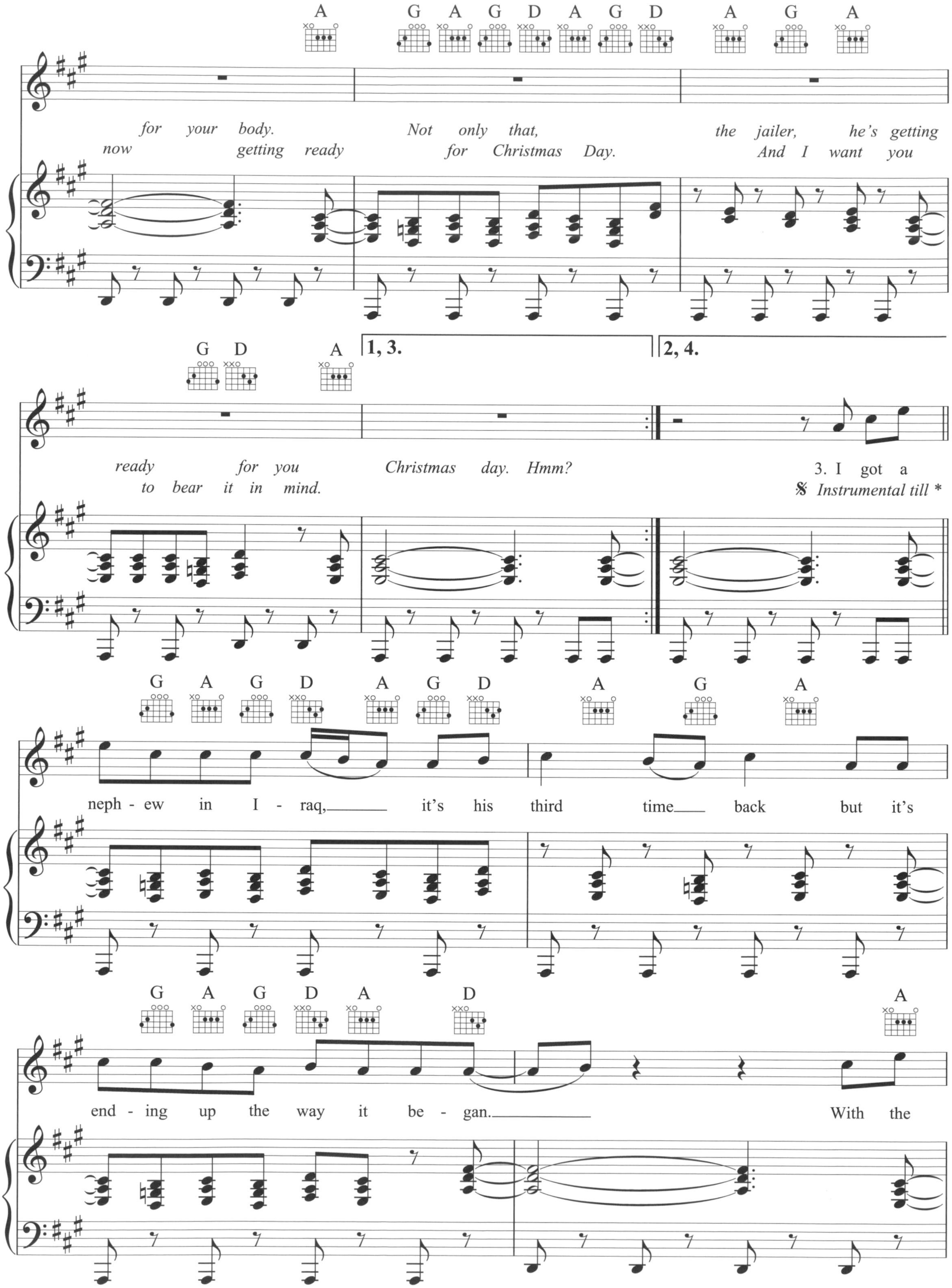
A G A G D A G D A G A
for your body. Not only that, the jailer, he's getting
now getting ready for Christmas Day. And I want you
G D A
1, 3.
2, 4.
ready for you Christmas day. Hmm?
to bear it in mind.
3. I got a
𝄋 Instrumental till *
G A G D A G D A G A
nephew in I - raq, it's his third time back but it's
G A G D A D A
end - ing up the way it be - gan. With the

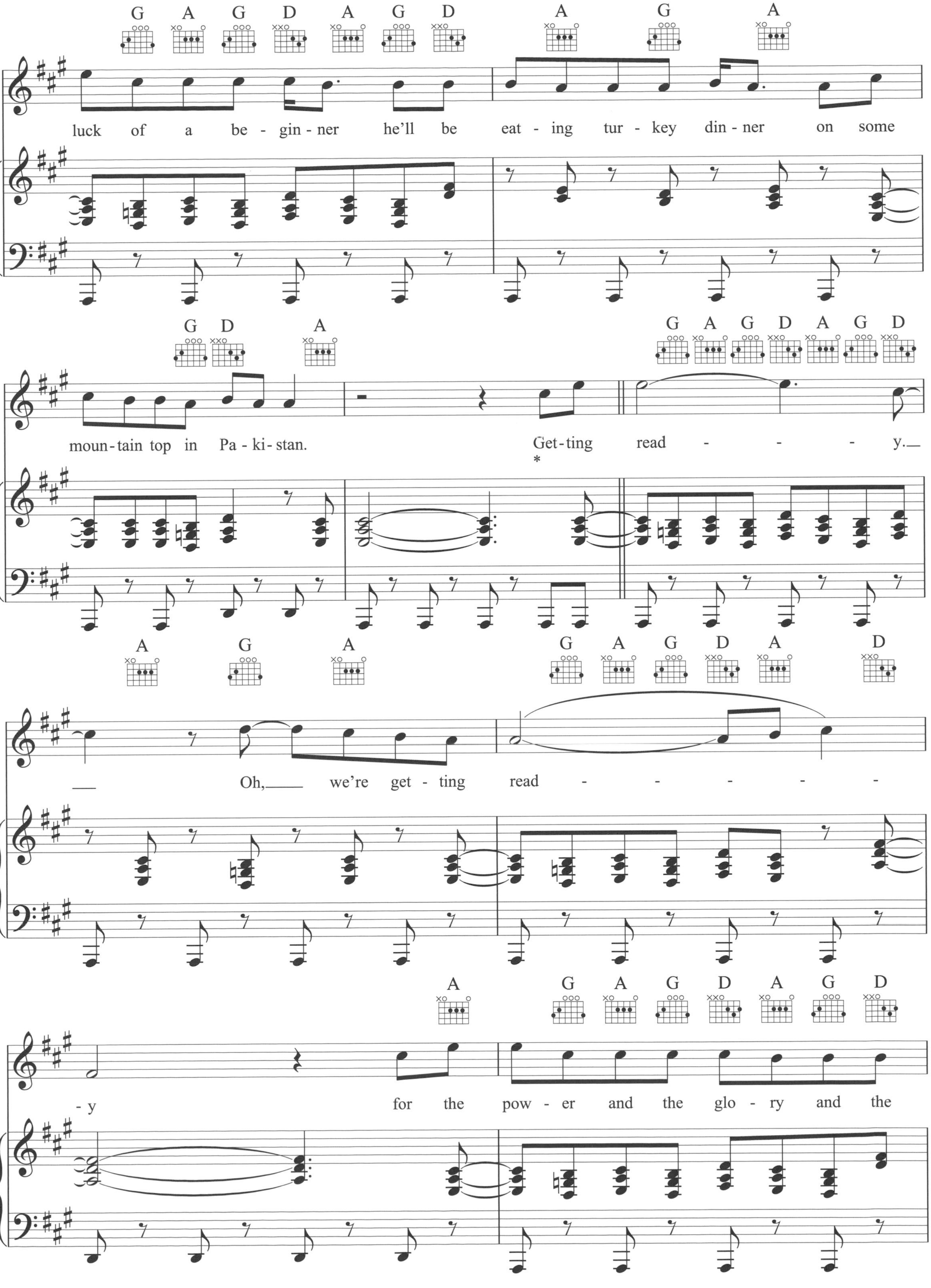
G A G D A G D A G A
luck of a be - gin - ner he'll be eat - ing tur - key din - ner on some
G D A G A G D A G D
moun - tain top in Pa - ki - stan. Get - ting read - - - - y.
*
A G A G A G D A D
Oh, we're get - ting read - - - - -
A G A G D A G D
- y for the pow - er and the glo - ry and the

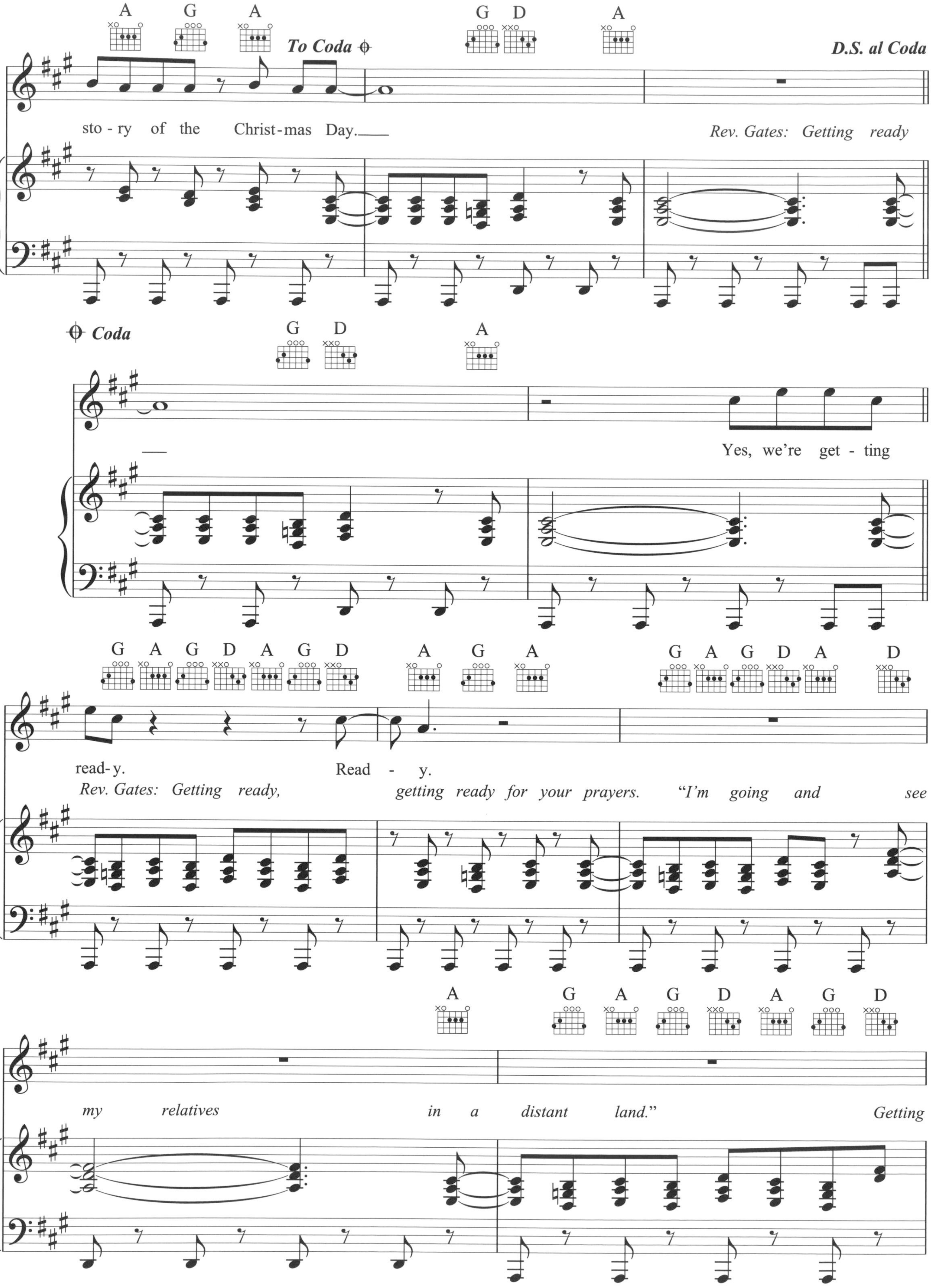
A G A
To Coda
G D A
D.S. al Coda
sto - ry of the Christ-mas Day.
Rev. Gates: Getting ready
Coda
G D A
Yes, we're get - ting
G A G D A G D A G A G A G D A D
read- y. Read - y.
Rev. Gates: Getting ready, getting ready for your prayers. "I'm going and see
A G A G D A G D
my relatives in a distant land."
Getting

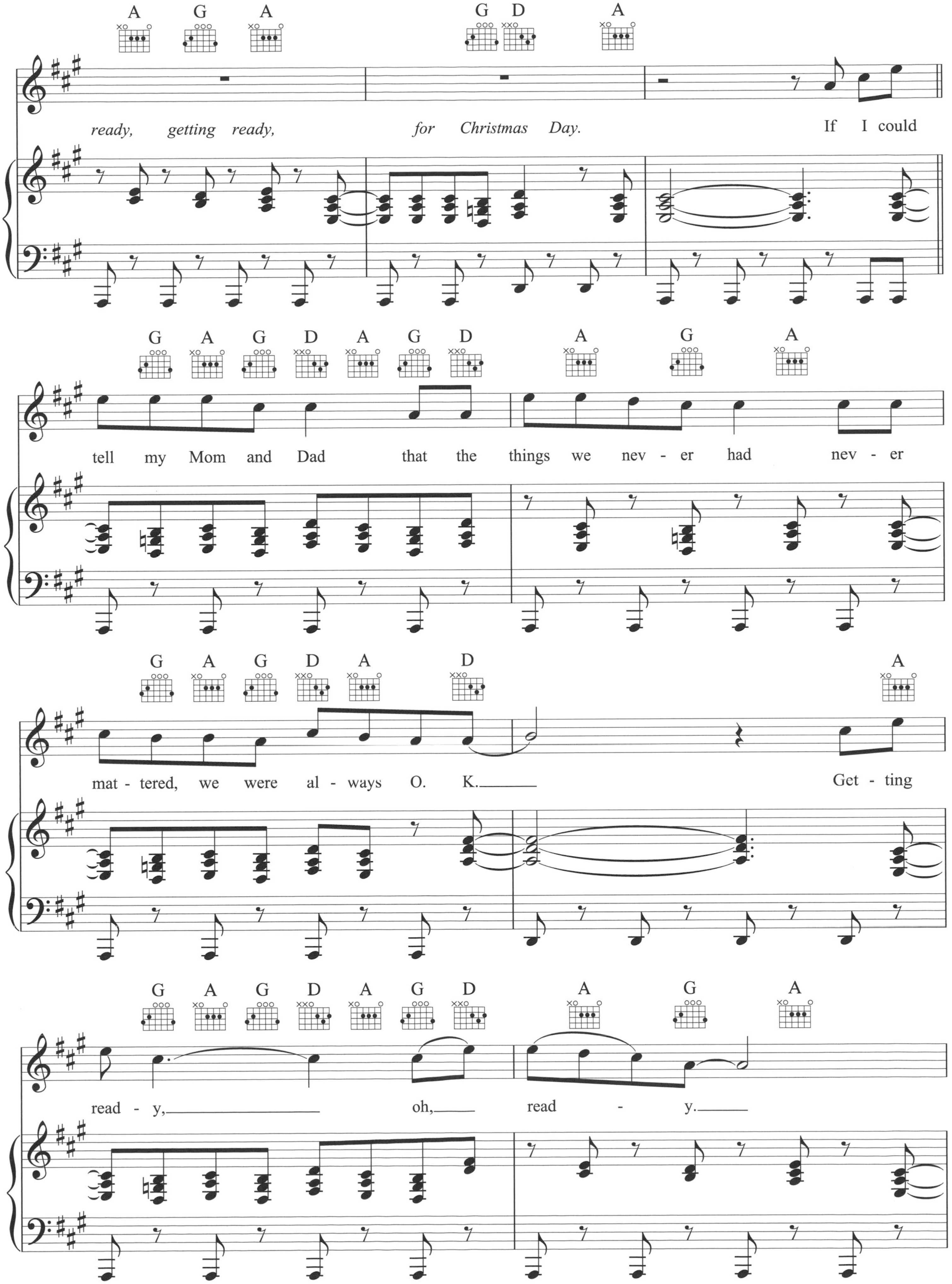
A G A G D A
ready, getting ready, for Christmas Day. If I could
G A G D A G D A G A
tell my Mom and Dad that the things we nev - er had nev - er
G A G D A D A
mat - tered, we were al - ways O. K. Get - ting
G A G D A G D A G A
read - y, oh, read - y.

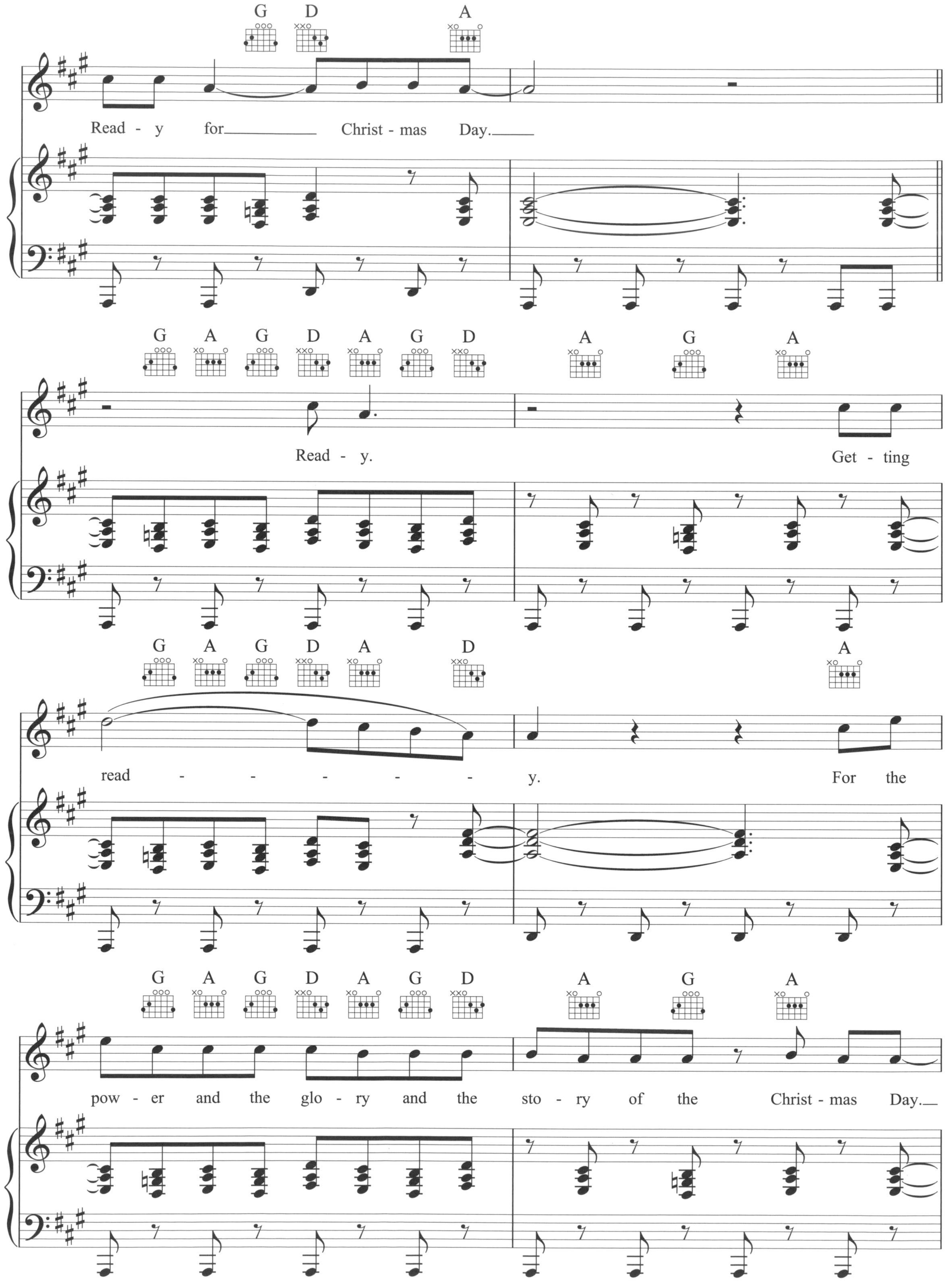
G D A
Read - y for Christ - mas Day.
G A G D A G D A G A
Read - y. Get - ting
G A G D A D A
read - - - - - y. For the
G A G D A G D A G A
pow - er and the glo - ry and the sto - ry of the Christ - mas Day.

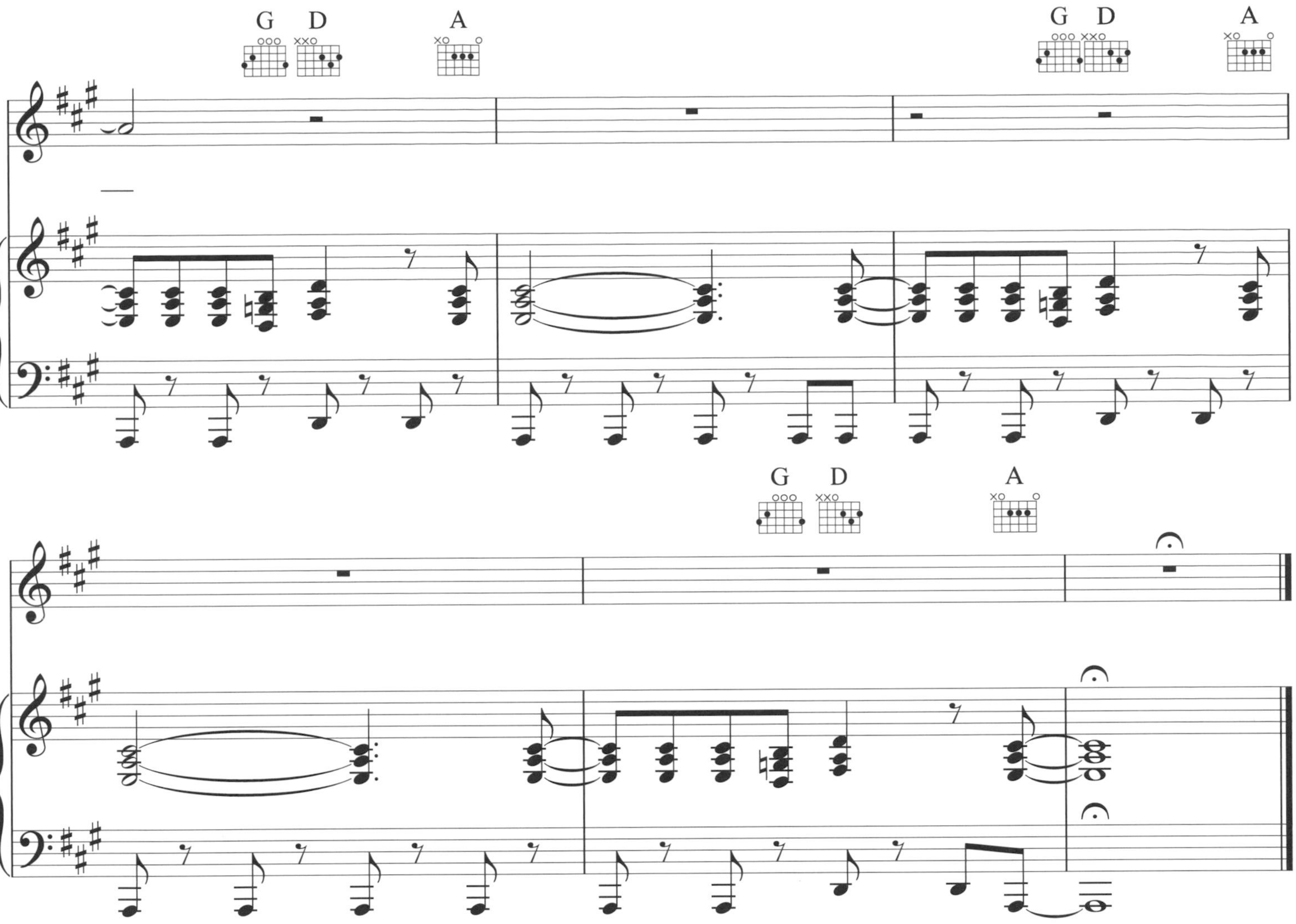

𝄋

Rev. Gates (spoken):

Getting ready for Christmas Day
Done made it up in your mind that I'm going
New York, Philadelphia, Chicago.
I'm going on a trip, getting ready for Christmas Day
But when Christmas come nobody knows where you'll be.
You might ask me
I may be layin' in some lonesome grave
Getting ready for Christmas Day.

The Afterlife

Words & Music by Paul Simon

♩ = 84
Repeat 4 times ad lib.
D♭ G♭ A♭m G♭ D♭ A♭m G♭ D♭
4fr
Guitar
Drums
Cont. sim.
1. Af - ter I'd died and the make-up had dried I went back to my place.
(2.) new kid in school got to fol - low the rule, you got to learn the rou - tine. Whoa! There's a
4. Af - ter you climb up the lad - der of time the Lord God is near.
3
No moon that night, but a heav - en - ly light shown on my face. Still I
girl o - ver there with the sun - shin - y hair, like a home-com - ing queen. I said "Hey,
Face to face in the vast - ness of space your words dis - ap - pear. And you

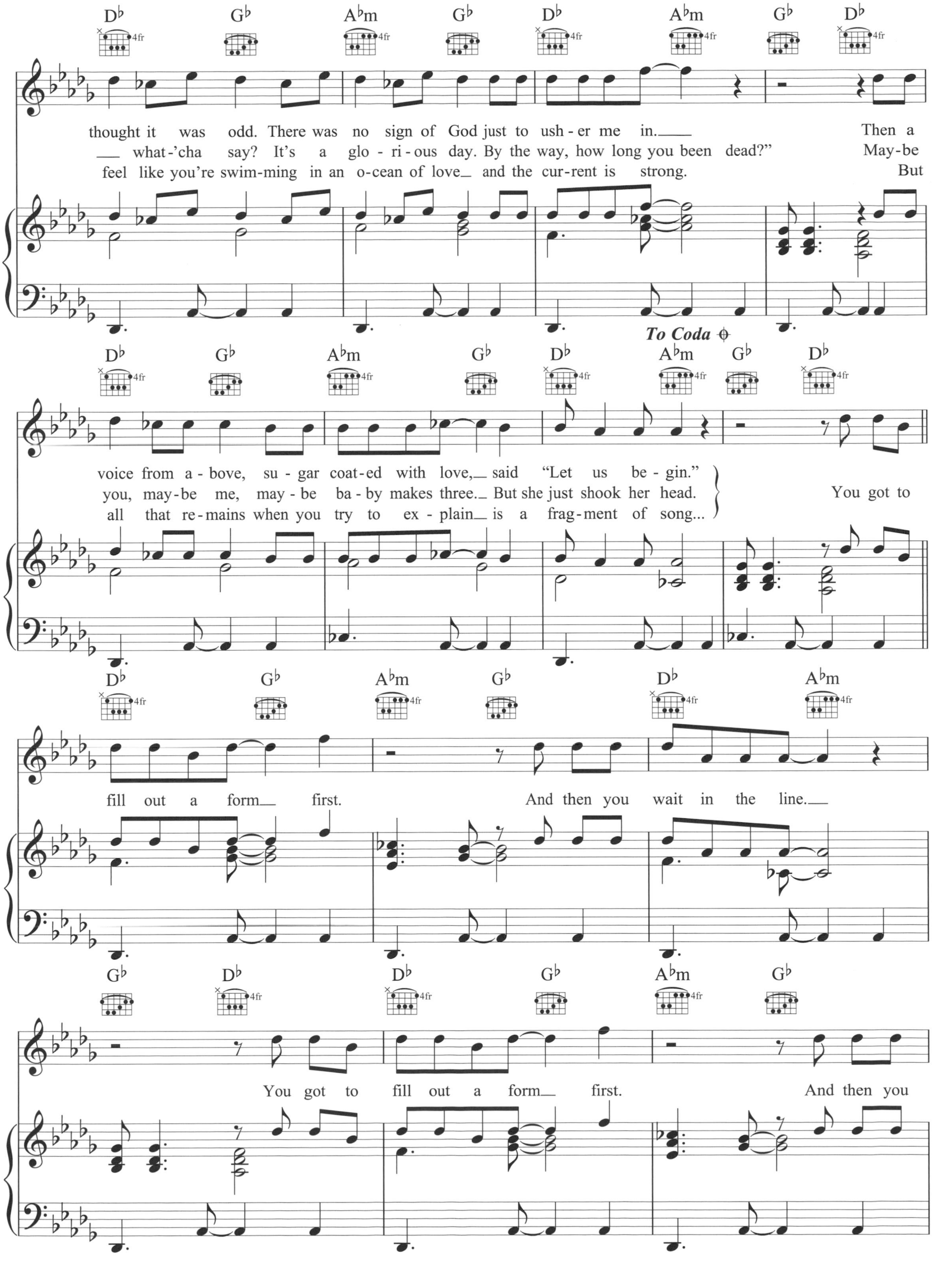
D♭ G♭ A♭m G♭ D♭ A♭m G♭ D♭
4fr
thought it was odd. There was no sign of God just to ush-er me in. Then a
what-'cha say? It's a glo-ri-ous day. By the way, how long you been dead?" May-be
feel like you're swim-ming in an o-cean of love and the cur-rent is strong. But
To Coda
voice from a-bove, su-gar coat-ed with love, said "Let us be-gin."
you, may-be me, may-be ba-by makes three. But she just shook her head. You got to
all that re-mains when you try to ex-plain is a frag-ment of song...
fill out a form first. And then you wait in the line.
You got to fill out a form first. And then you

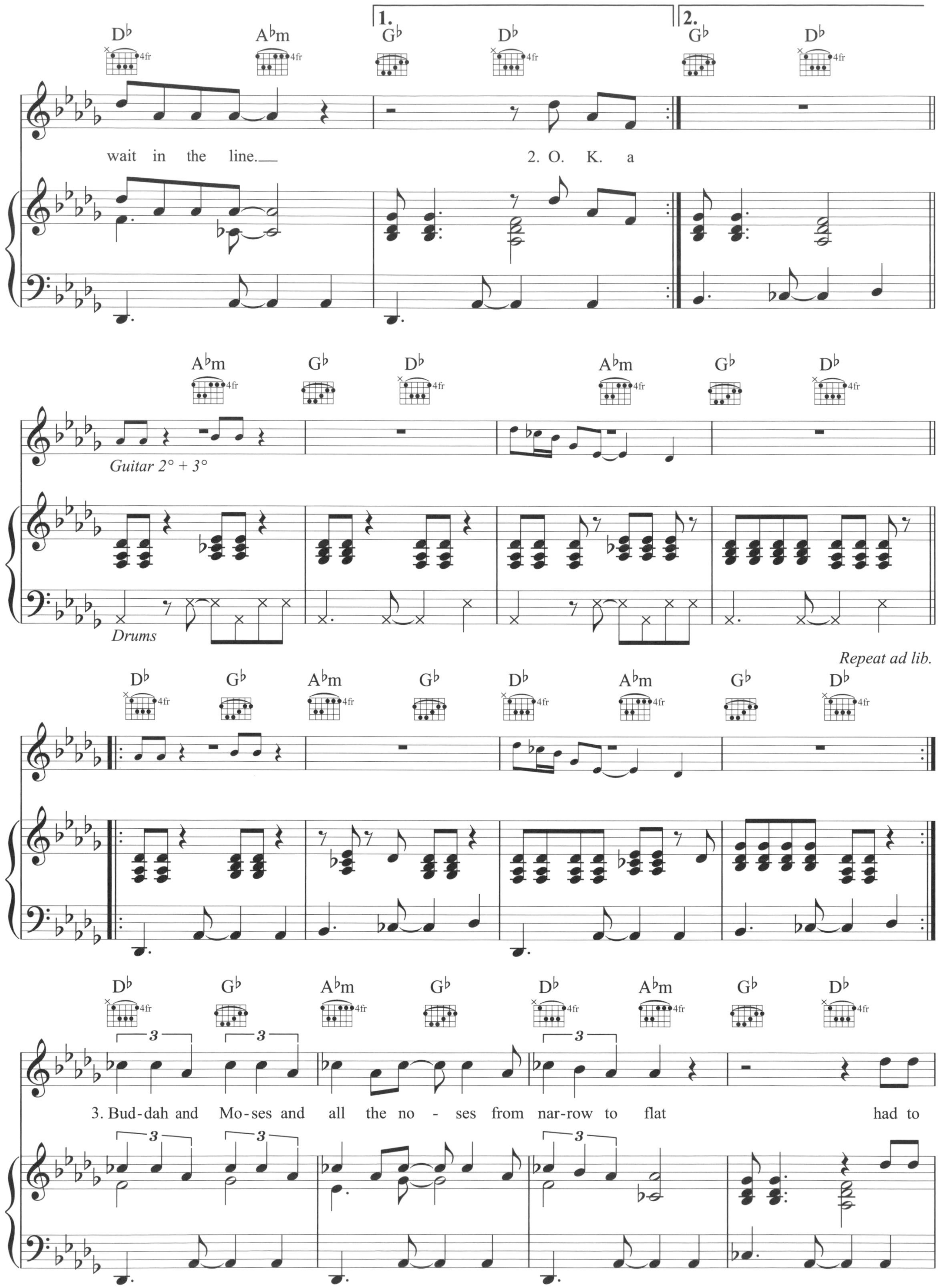
1.
2.
D♭ A♭m G♭ D♭ G♭ D♭
4fr
wait in the line.
2. O. K. a
Guitar 2° + 3°
Drums
Repeat ad lib.
3. Bud-dah and Mo-ses and all the no - ses from nar-row to flat had to

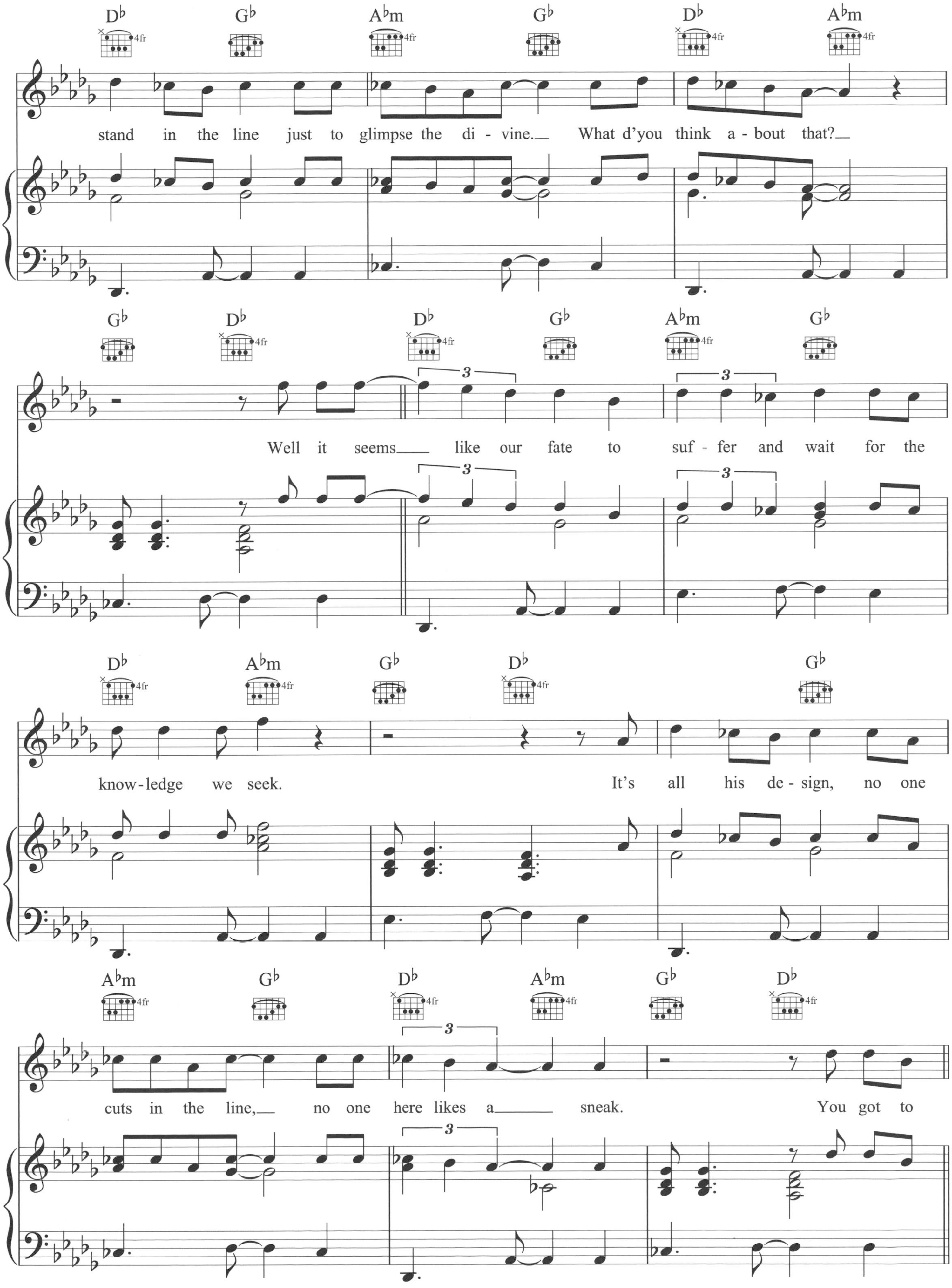
D♭ G♭ A♭m G♭ D♭ A♭m
stand in the line just to glimpse the di - vine. What d'you think a - bout that?
G♭ D♭ D♭ G♭ A♭m G♭
Well it seems like our fate to suf - fer and wait for the
D♭ A♭m G♭ D♭ G♭
know - ledge we seek. It's all his de - sign, no one
A♭m G♭ D♭ A♭m G♭ D♭
cuts in the line, no one here likes a sneak. You got to

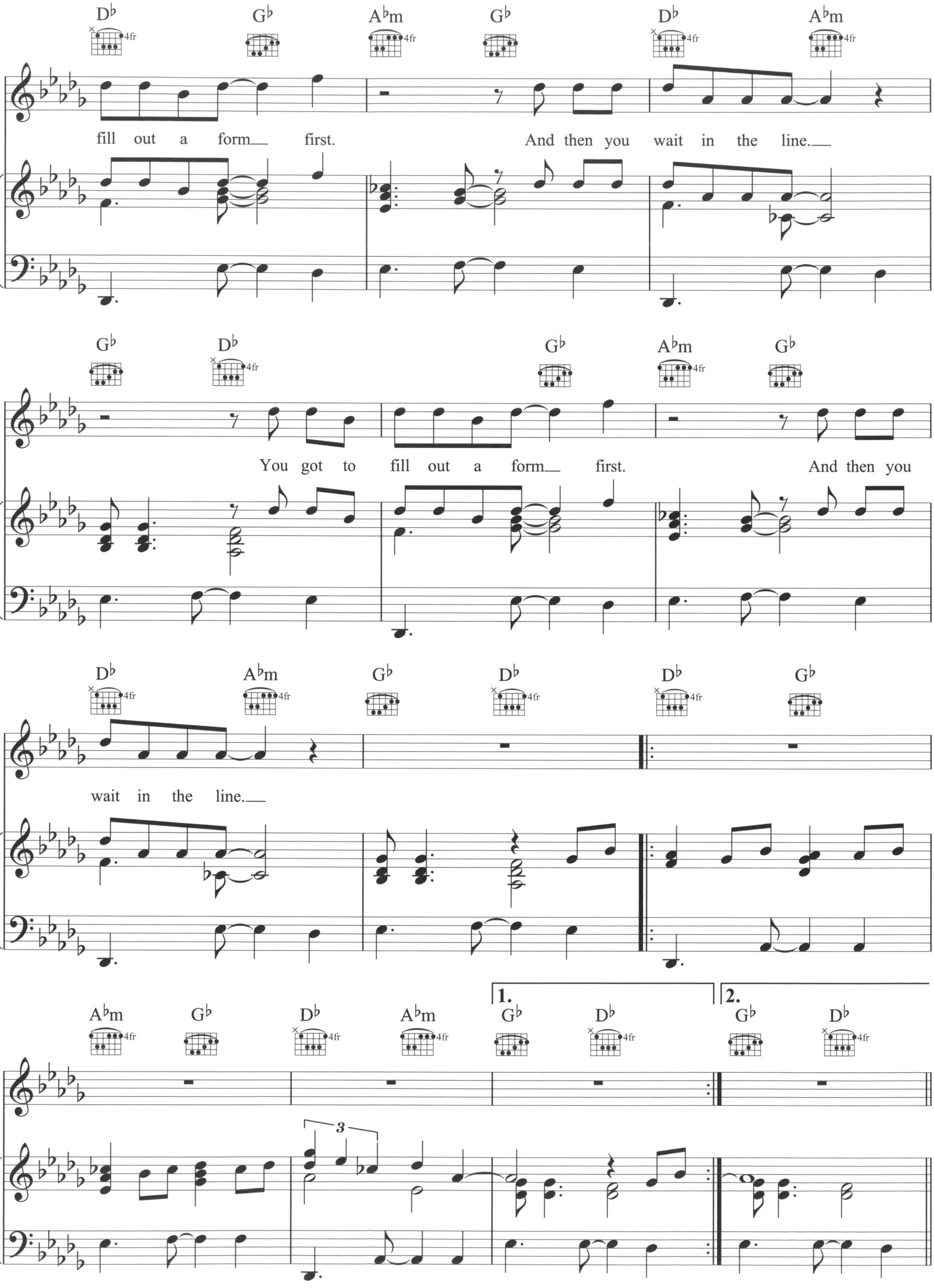
D♭ G♭ A♭m G♭ D♭ A♭m
fill out a form first. And then you wait in the line.
G♭ D♭ G♭ A♭m G♭
You got to fill out a form first. And then you
D♭ A♭m G♭ D♭ D♭ G♭
wait in the line.
A♭m G♭ D♭ A♭m
1. G♭ D♭
2. G♭ D♭
4fr
3

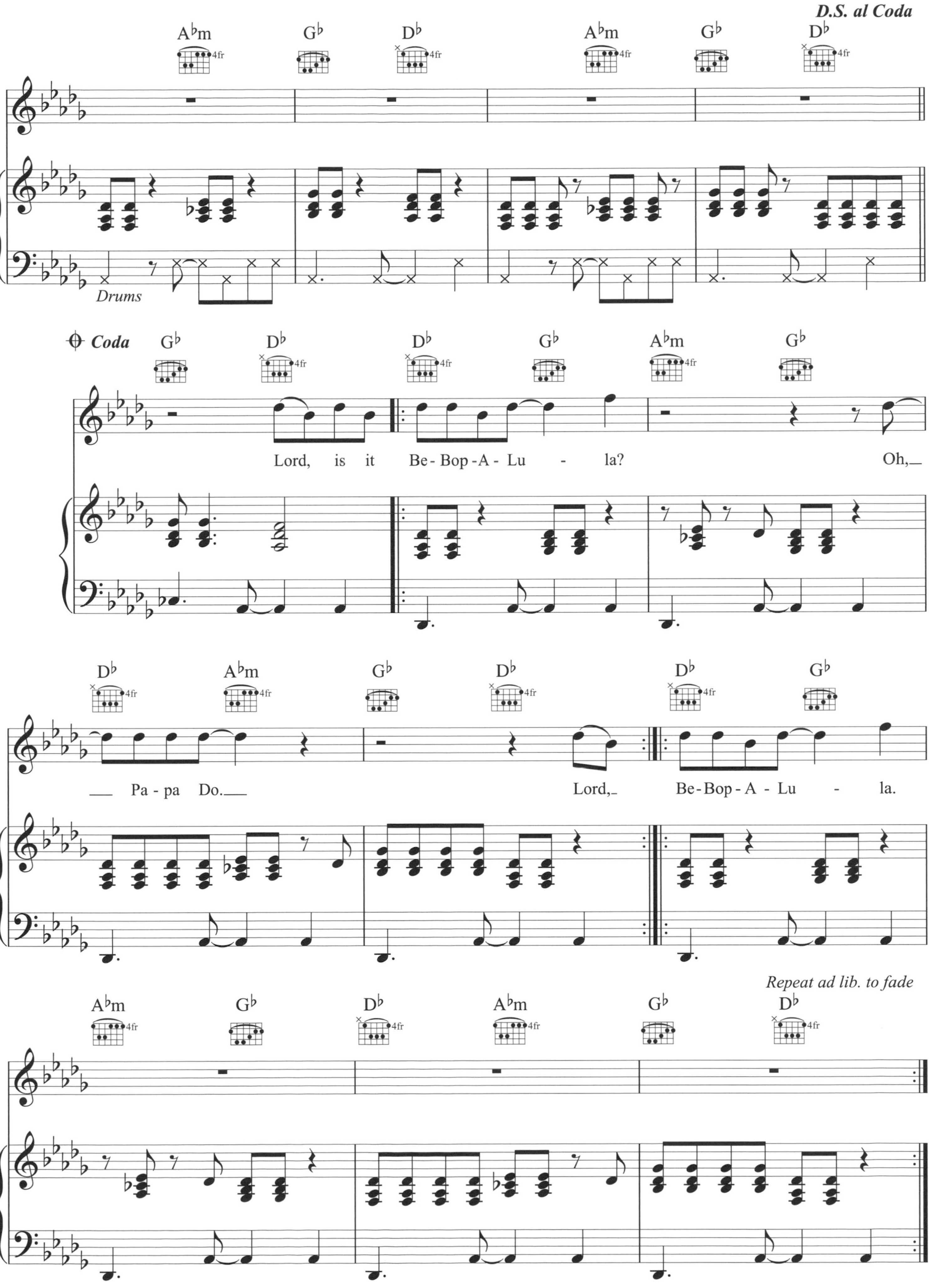
D.S. al Coda
A♭m G♭ D♭ A♭m G♭ D♭
4fr 4fr 4fr 4fr
Drums
Coda G♭ D♭ D♭ G♭ A♭m G♭
Lord, is it Be-Bop-A-Lu - la? Oh,
D♭ A♭m G♭ D♭ D♭ G♭
Papa Do. Lord, Be-Bop-A-Lu - la.
Repeat ad lib. to fade
A♭m G♭ D♭ A♭m G♭ D♭

Dazzling Blue

Words & Music by Paul Simon

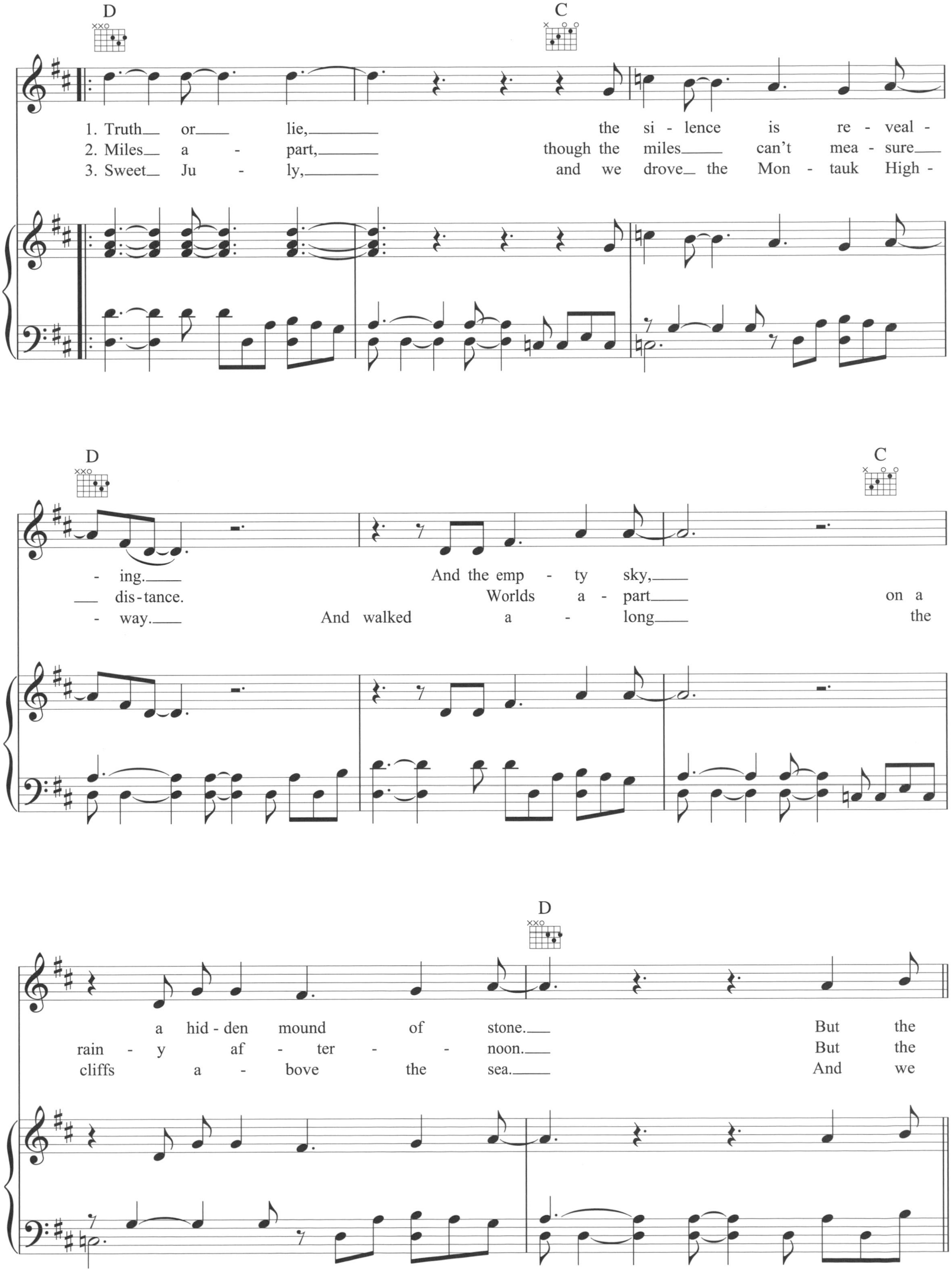
D
C
1. Truth or lie, the si - lence is re - veal -
2. Miles a - part, though the miles can't mea - sure
3. Sweet Ju - ly, and we drove the Mon - tauk High -
D
C
- ing. And the emp - ty sky,
dis - tance. Worlds a - part on a
- way. And walked a - long the
D
a hid - den mound of stone. But the
rain - y af - ter - noon. But the
cliffs a - bove the sea. And we

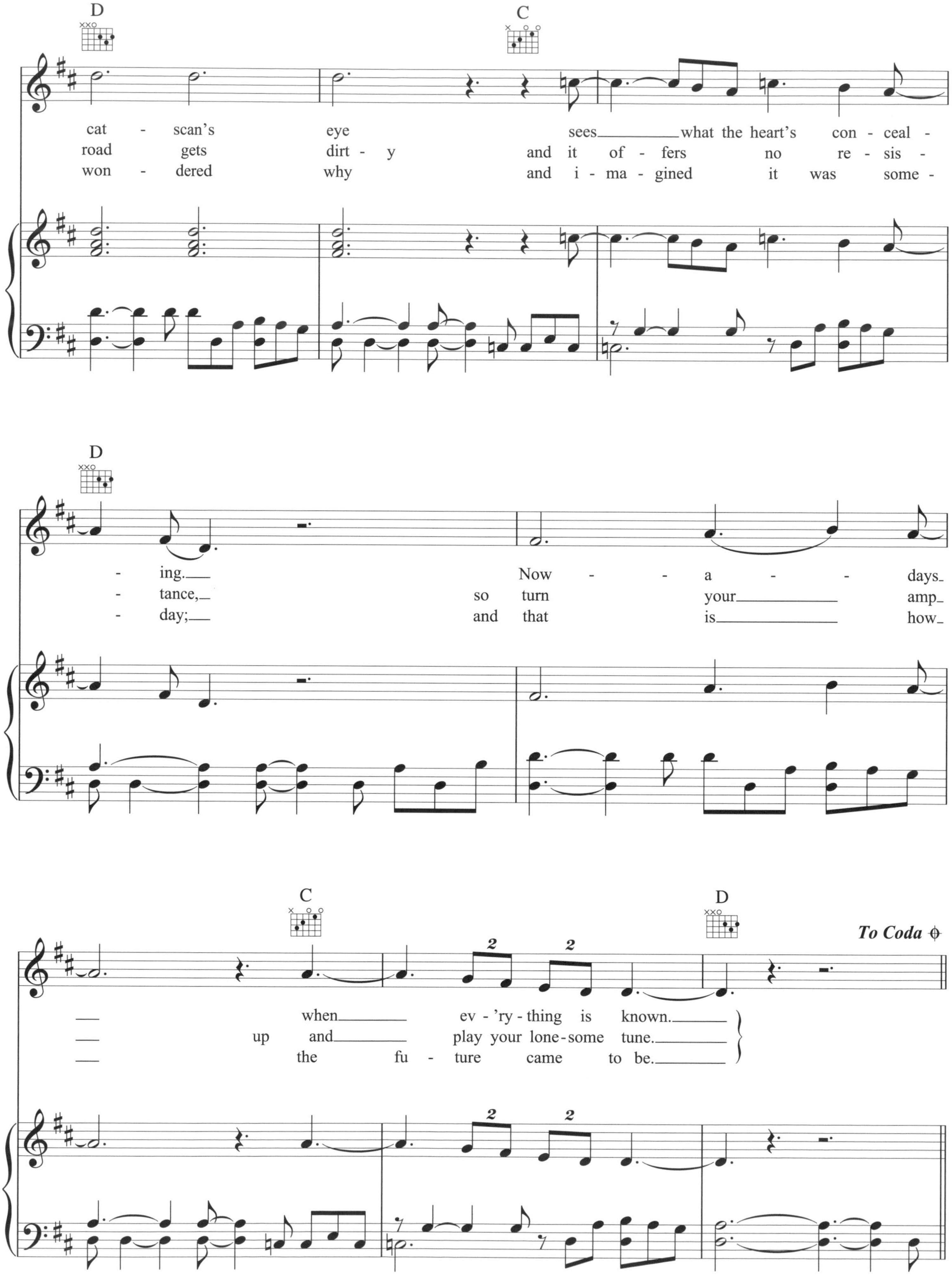
D
C
cat - scan's eye sees what the heart's con - ceal -
road gets dirt - y and it of - fers no re - sis -
won - dered why and i - ma - gined it was some -
D
- ing. Now - - a - - days
- tance, so turn your amp
- day; and that is how
C
D
To Coda
when ev - 'ry - thing is known.
up and play your lone - some tune.
the fu - ture came to be.

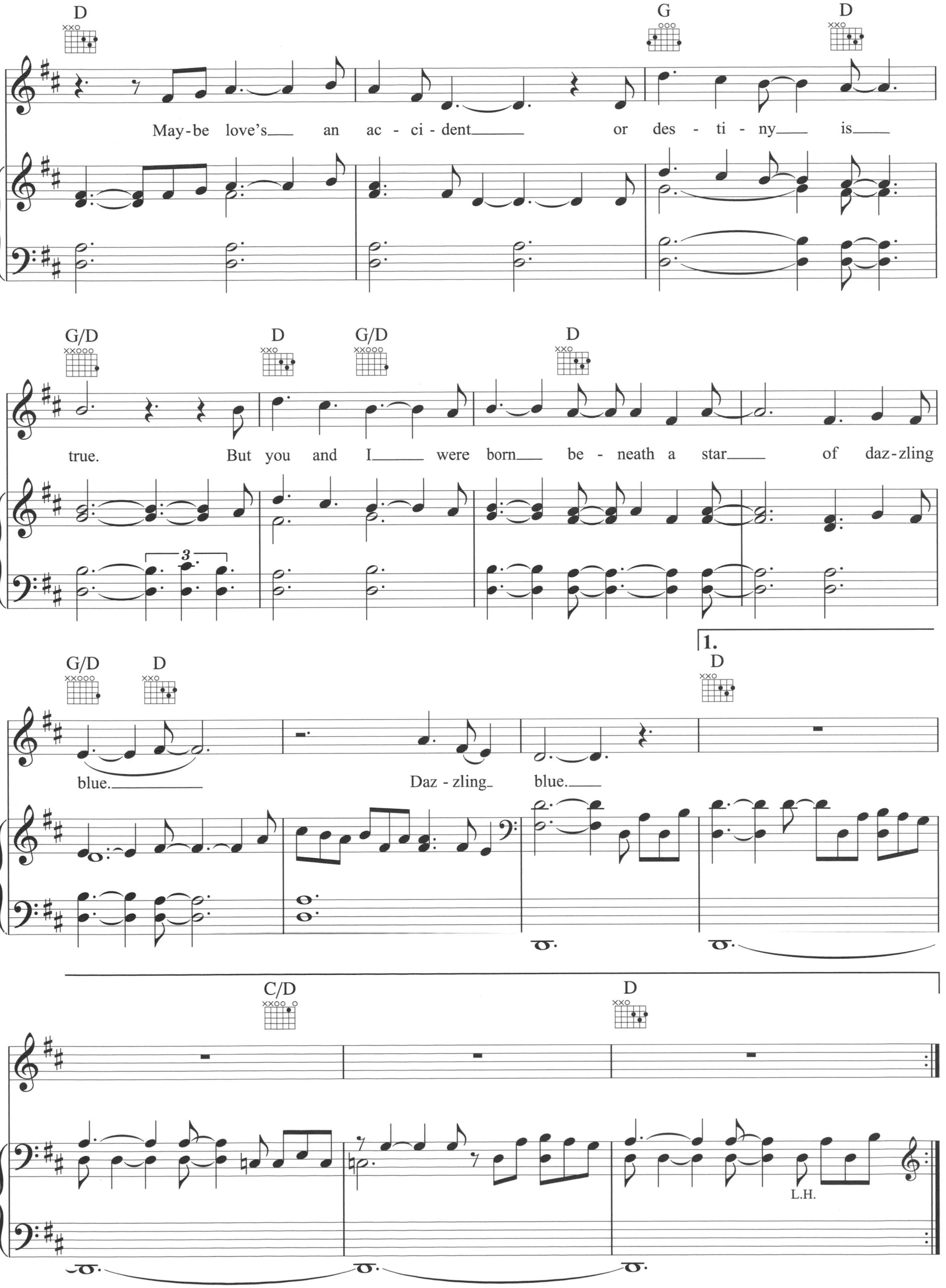
D
G
D
May-be love's an ac-ci-dent or des-ti-ny is
G/D
D
G/D
D
true. But you and I were born be-neath a star of daz-zling
3
G/D
D
1.
D
blue. Daz-zling blue.
C/D
D
L.H.

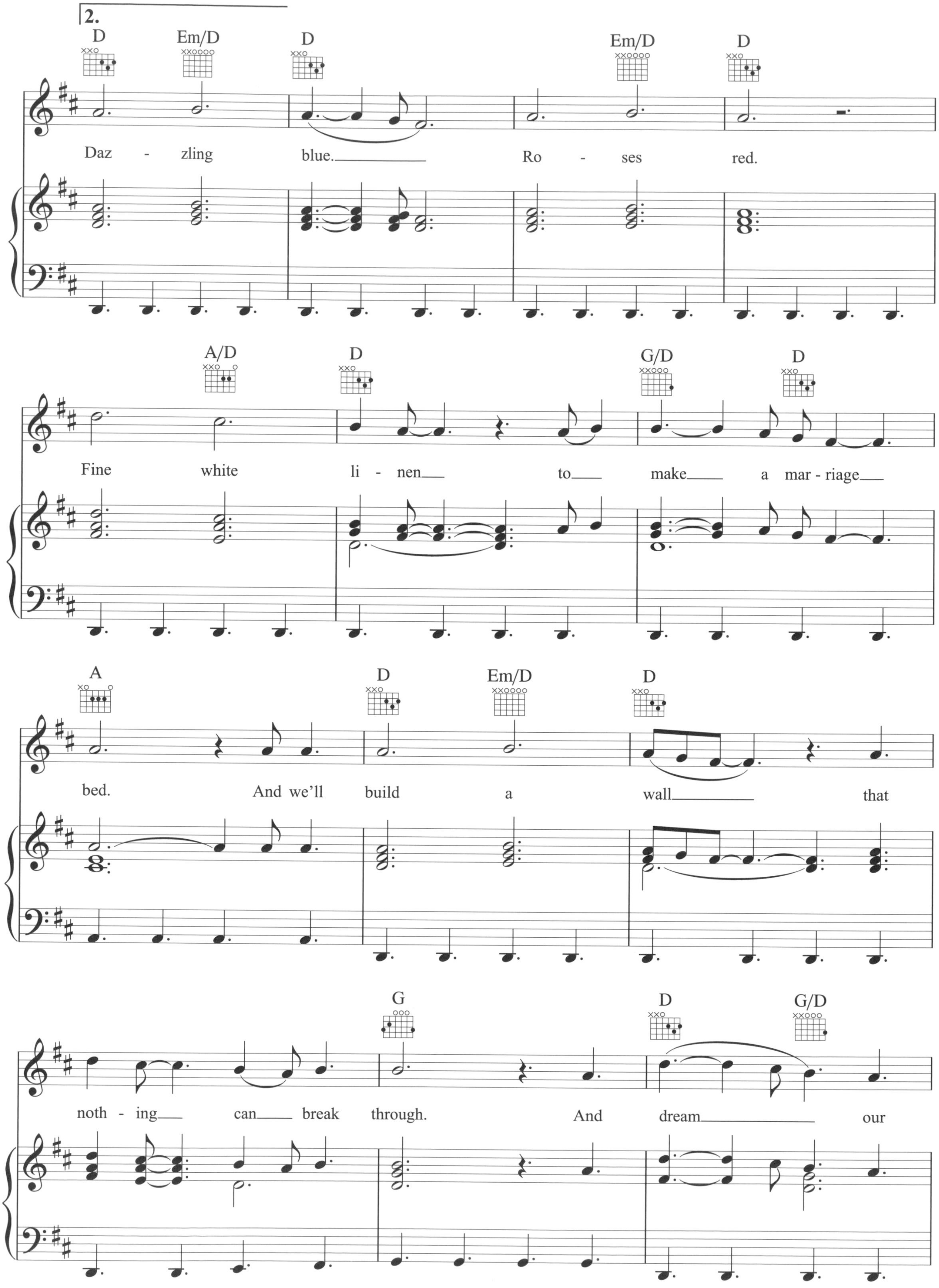
2.
D Em/D D Em/D D
Daz - zling blue. Ro - ses red.
A/D D G/D D
Fine white li - nen to make a mar - riage
A D Em/D D
bed. And we'll build a wall that
G D G/D
noth - ing can break through. And dream our

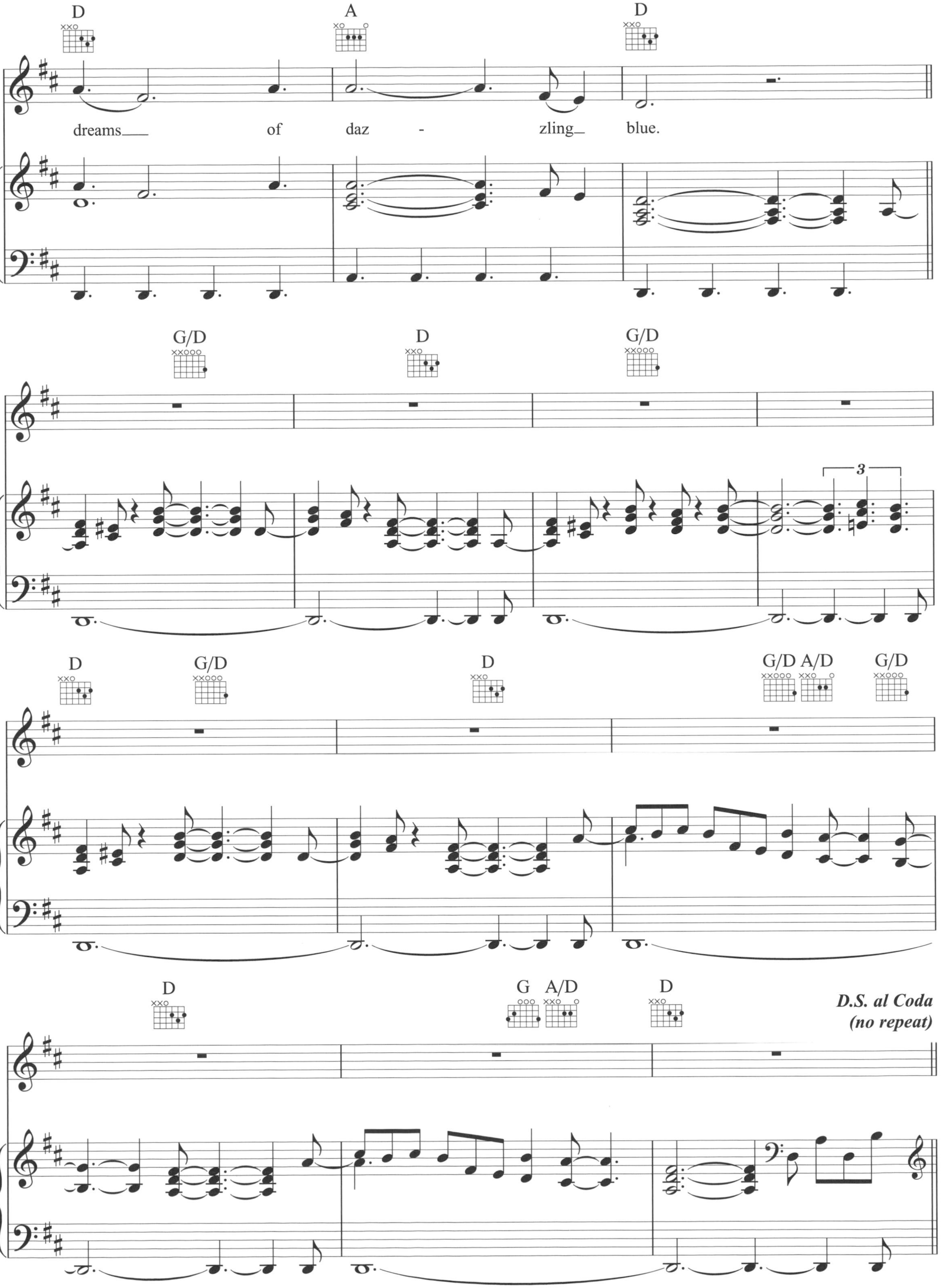
D
A
D
dreams___ of daz - zling_ blue.
G/D
D
G/D
D
G/D
D
G/D A/D G/D
D
G A/D
D
D.S. al Coda
(no repeat)
3

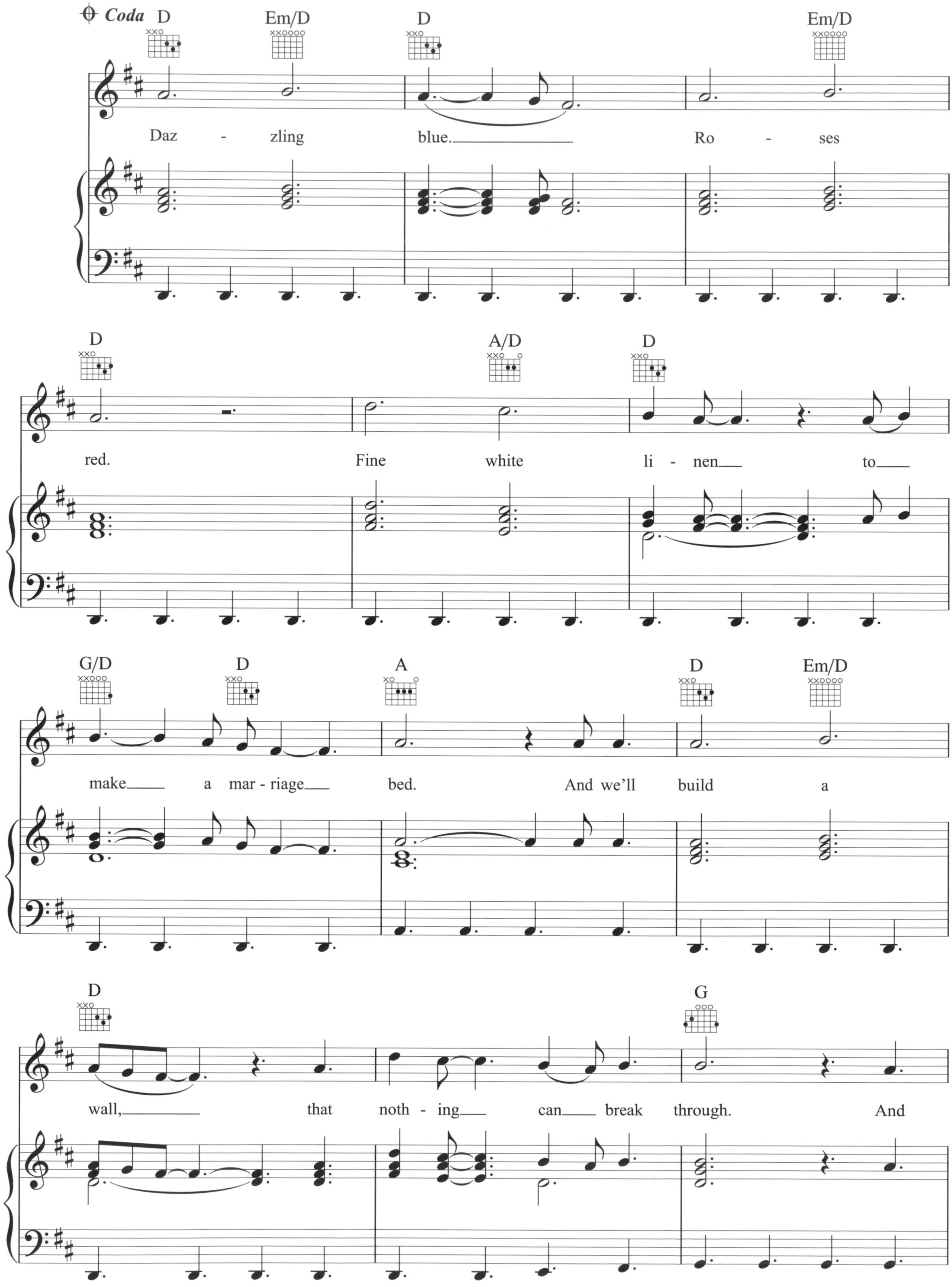
Coda
D Em/D D Em/D
Daz - zling blue. Ro - ses
D A/D D
red. Fine white li - nen to
G/D D A D Em/D
make a mar - riage bed. And we'll build a
D G
wall, that noth - ing can break through. And

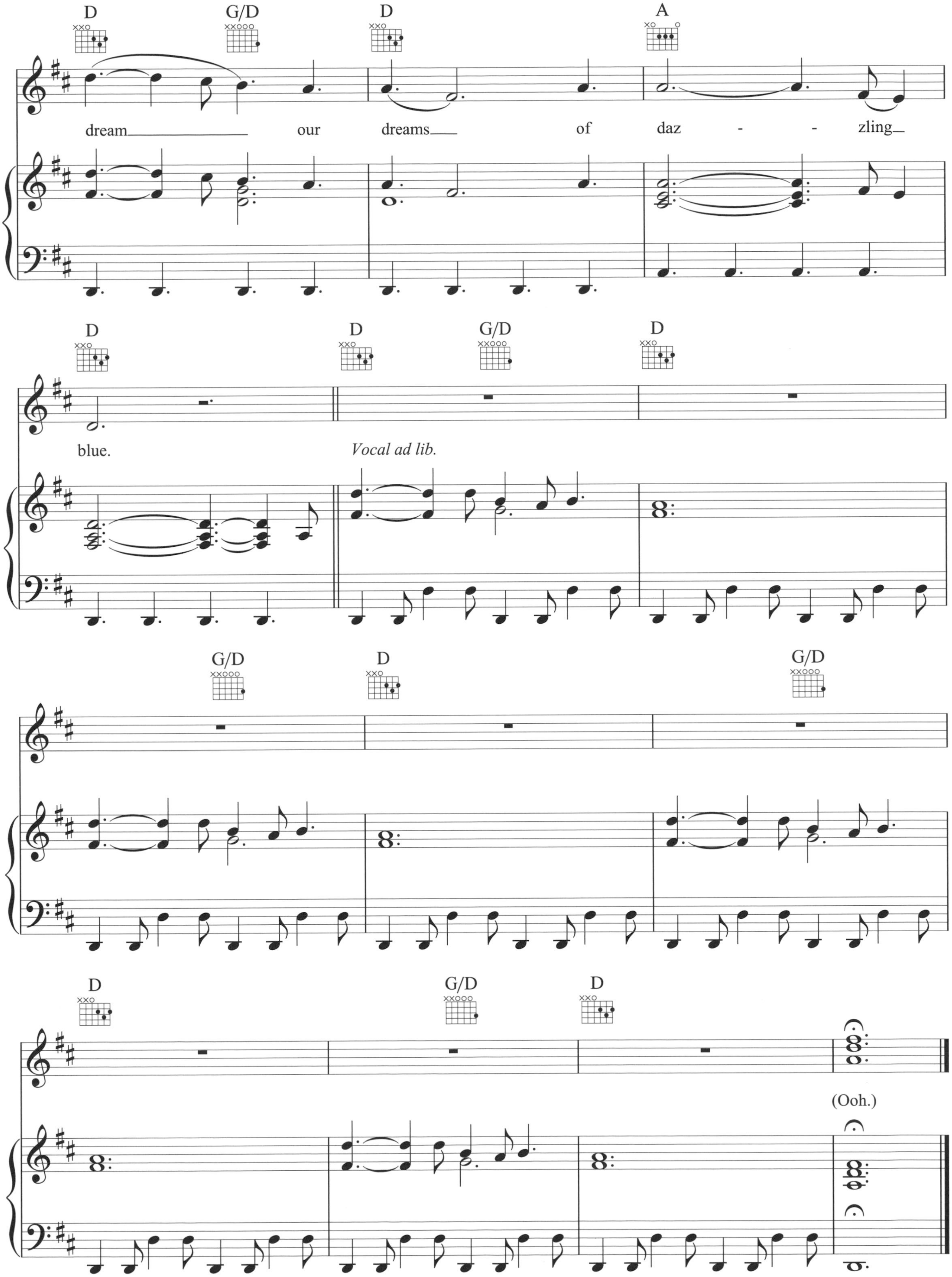
D
G/D
D
A
dream our dreams of daz - - zling
D
D
G/D
D
blue.
Vocal ad lib.
G/D
D
G/D
D
G/D
D
(Ooh.)

Rewrite

Words & Music by Paul Simon

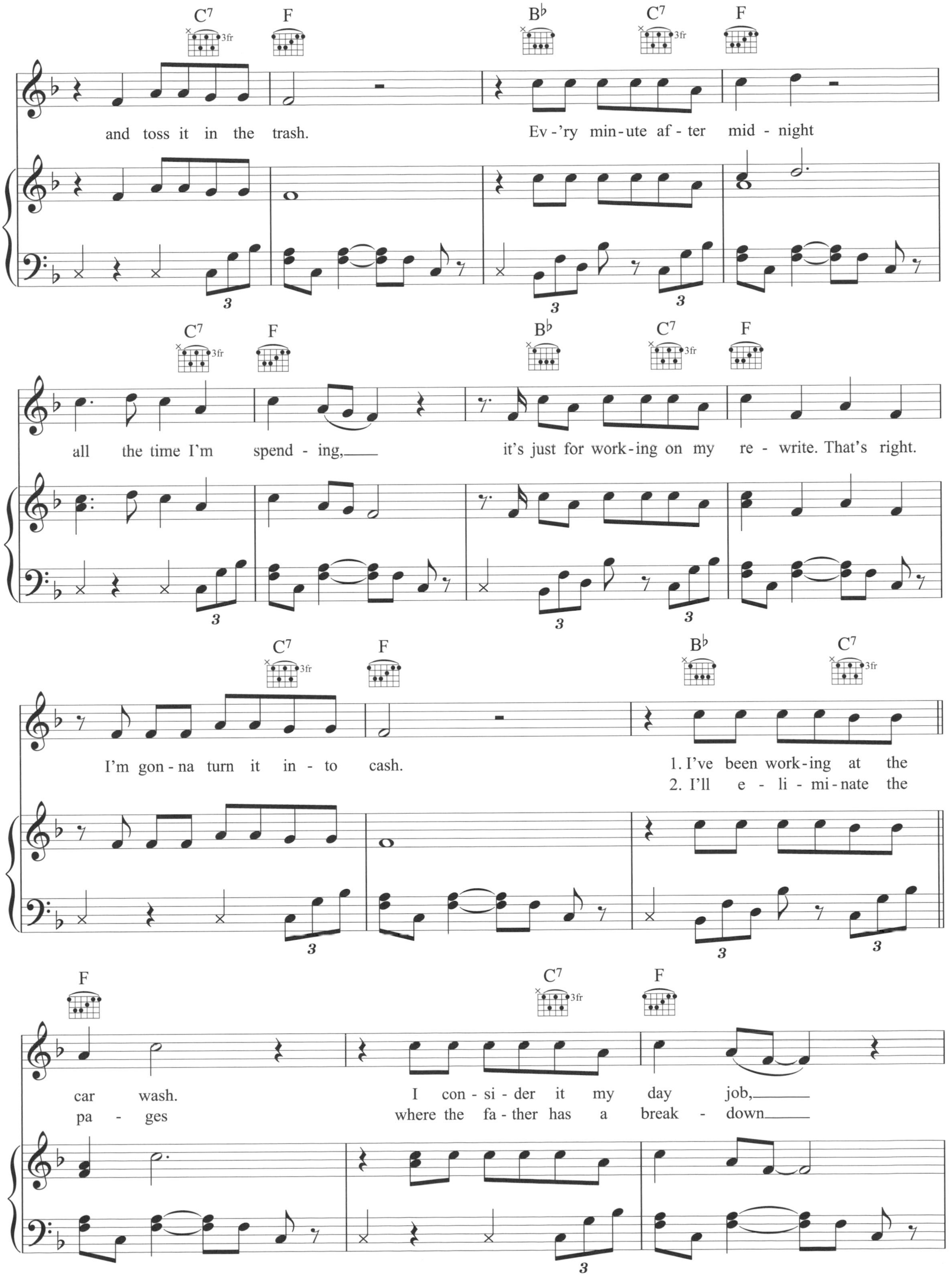
C7 F B♭ C7 F
and toss it in the trash.
Ev-'ry min-ute af-ter mid-night
C7 F B♭ C7 F
all the time I'm spend-ing,
it's just for work-ing on my re-write. That's right.
C7 F B♭ C7
I'm gon-na turn it in-to cash.
1. I've been work-ing at the
2. I'll e-li-mi-nate the
F C7 F
car wash.
I con-si-der it my day job,
pa-ges
where the fa-ther has a break-down
3fr

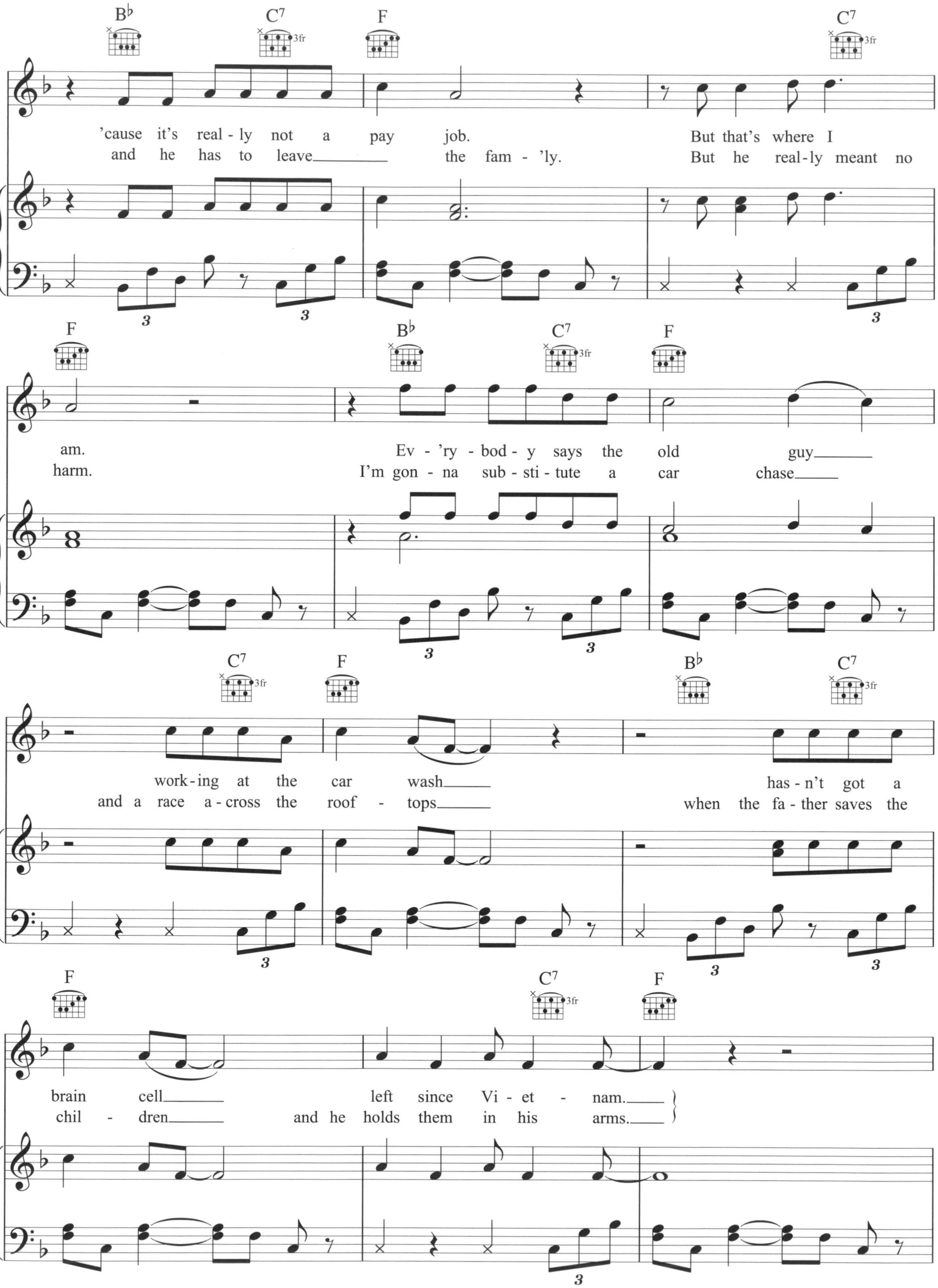
B♭ C7 F C7
'cause it's real - ly not a pay job. But that's where I
and he has to leave the fam - 'ly. But he real - ly meant no
F B♭ C7 F
am. Ev - 'ry - bod - y says the old guy
harm. I'm gon - na sub - sti - tute a car chase
C7 F B♭ C7
work - ing at the car wash has - n't got a
and a race a - cross the roof - tops when the fa - ther saves the
F C7 F
brain cell left since Vi - et - nam.
chil - dren and he holds them in his arms.

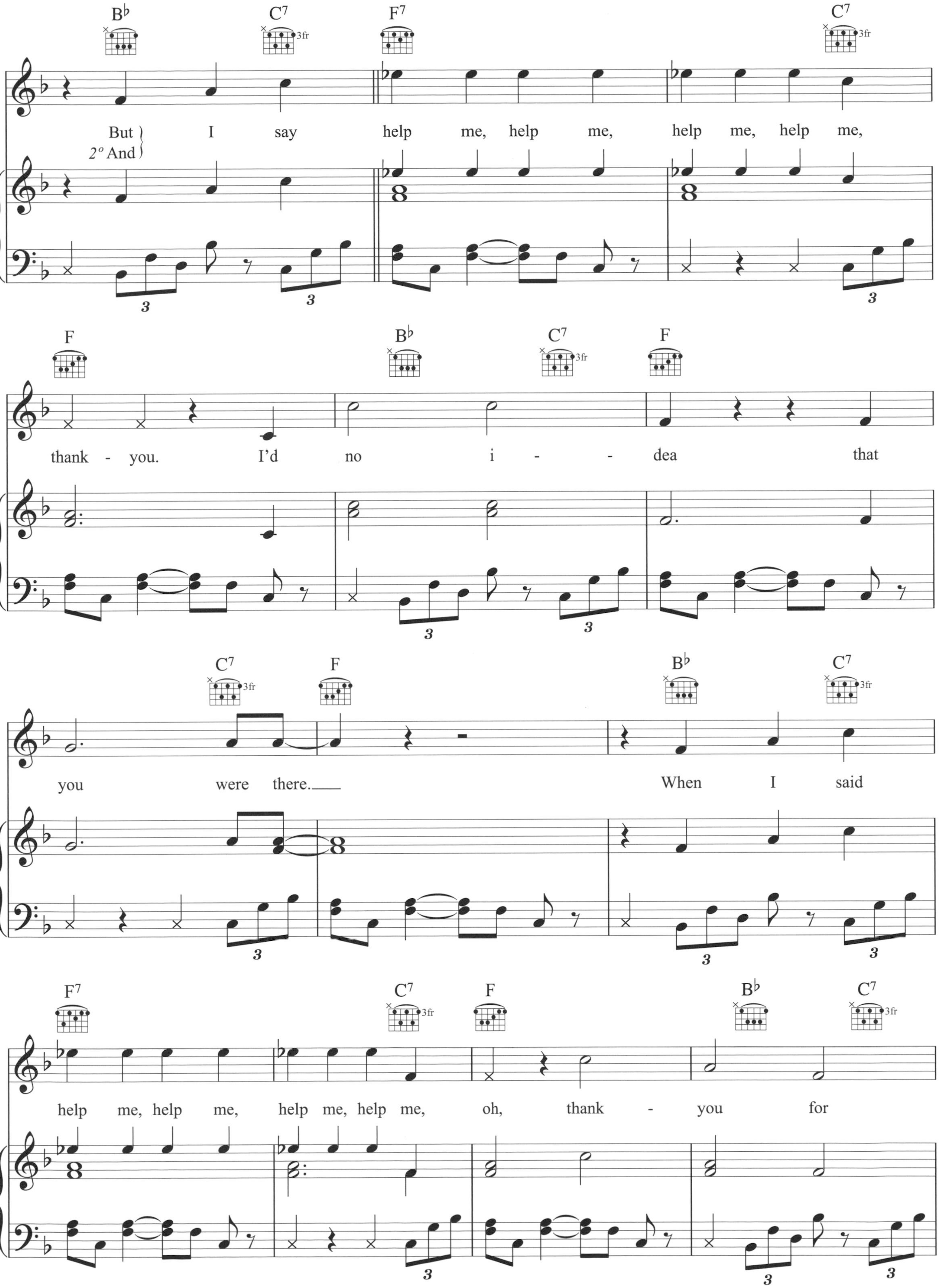
B♭ C7 F7 C7
But } I say help me, help me, help me, help me,
2º And }
F B♭ C7 F
thank - you. I'd no i - - dea that
C7 F B♭ C7
you were there.___ When I said
F7 C7 F B♭ C7
help me, help me, help me, help me, oh, thank - you for

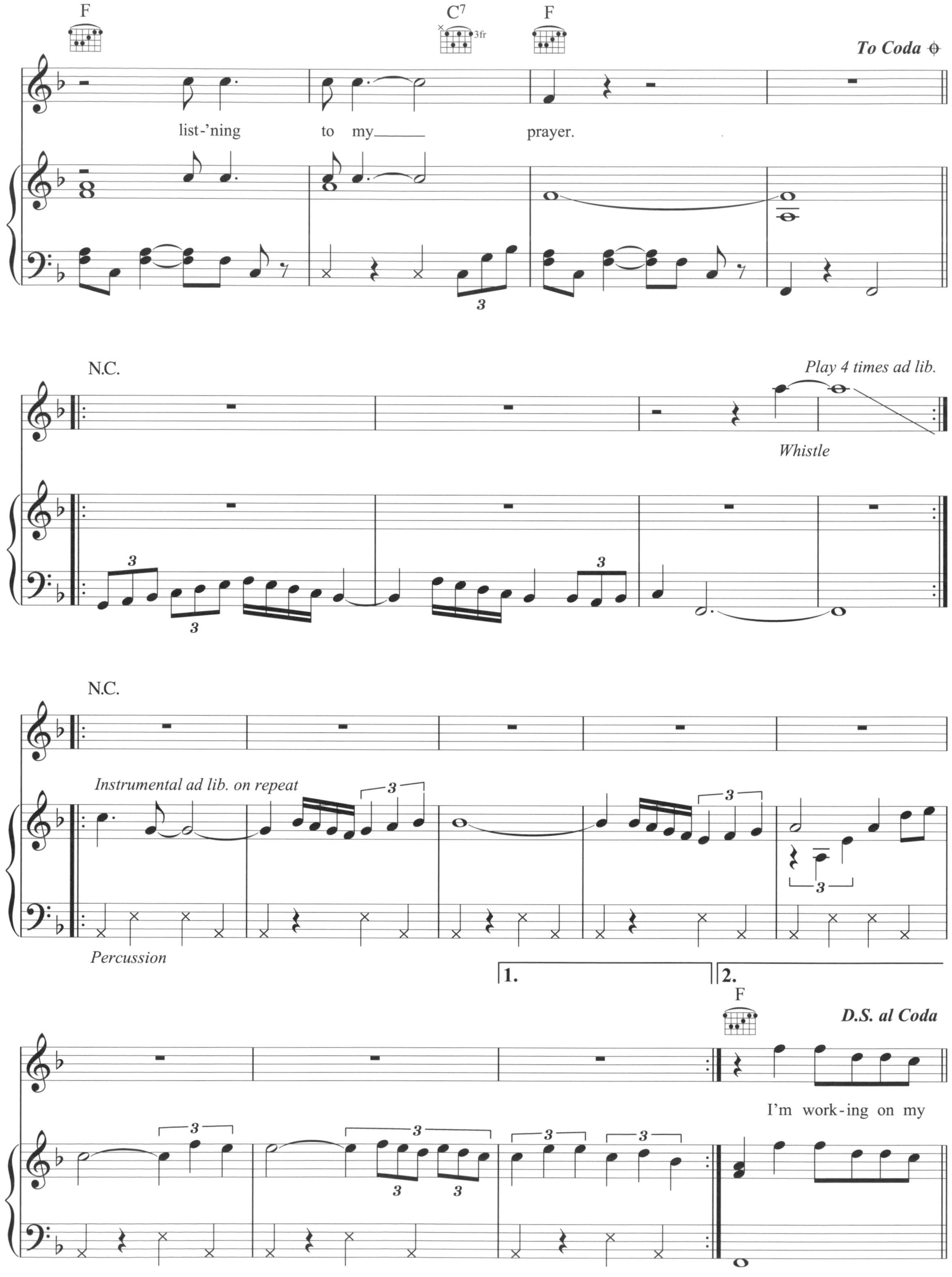
F
C7
3fr
F
To Coda
list-'ning
to my
prayer.
N.C.
Play 4 times ad lib.
Whistle
N.C.
Instrumental ad lib. on repeat
Percussion
1.
2.
F
D.S. al Coda
I'm work-ing on my

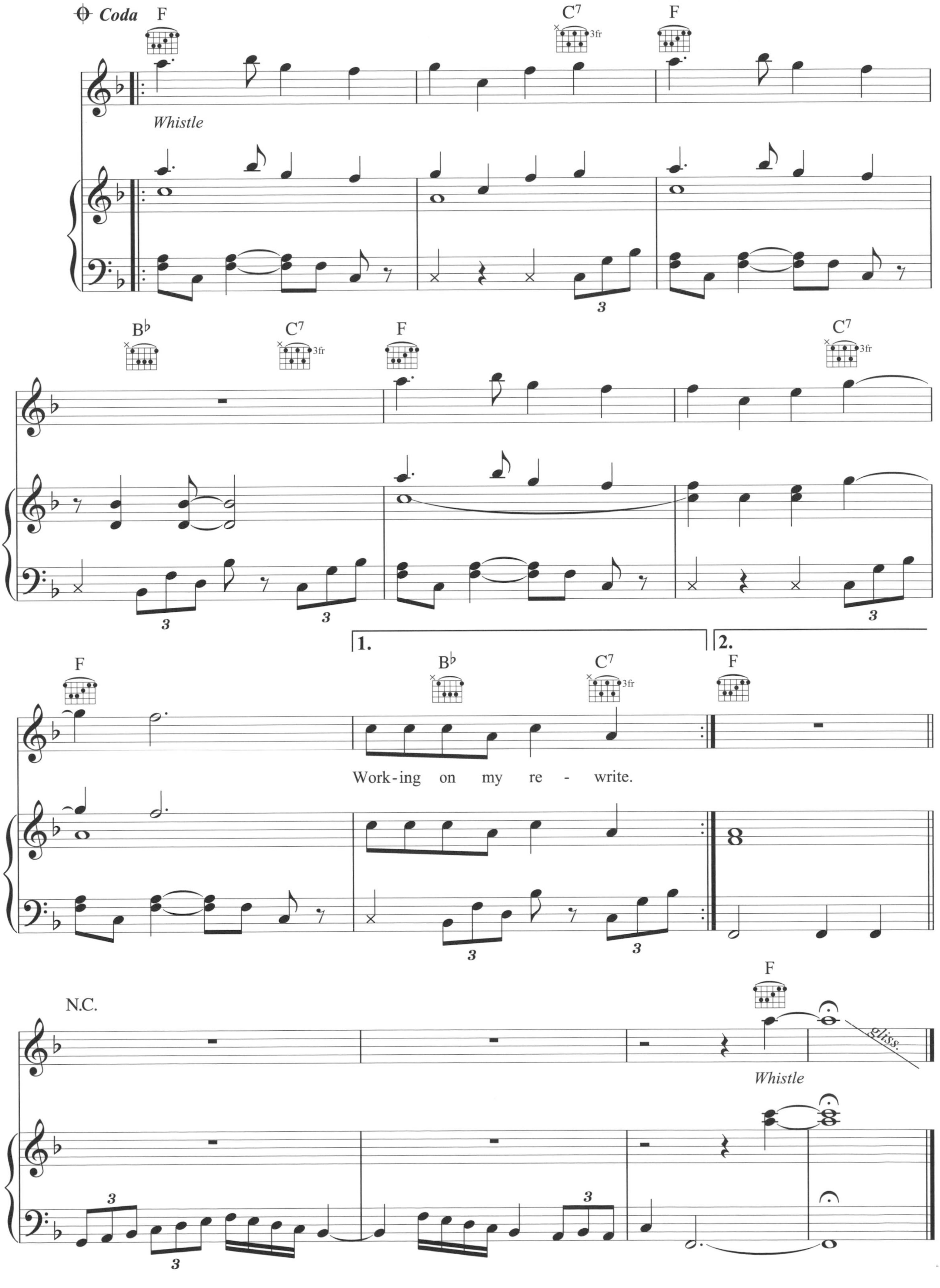
Coda
F
C7
F
Whistle
B♭
C7
F
C7
F
1.
B♭
C7
2.
F
Work-ing on my re - write.
N.C.
F
gliss.
Whistle

Love and Hard Times

Words & Music by Paul Simon

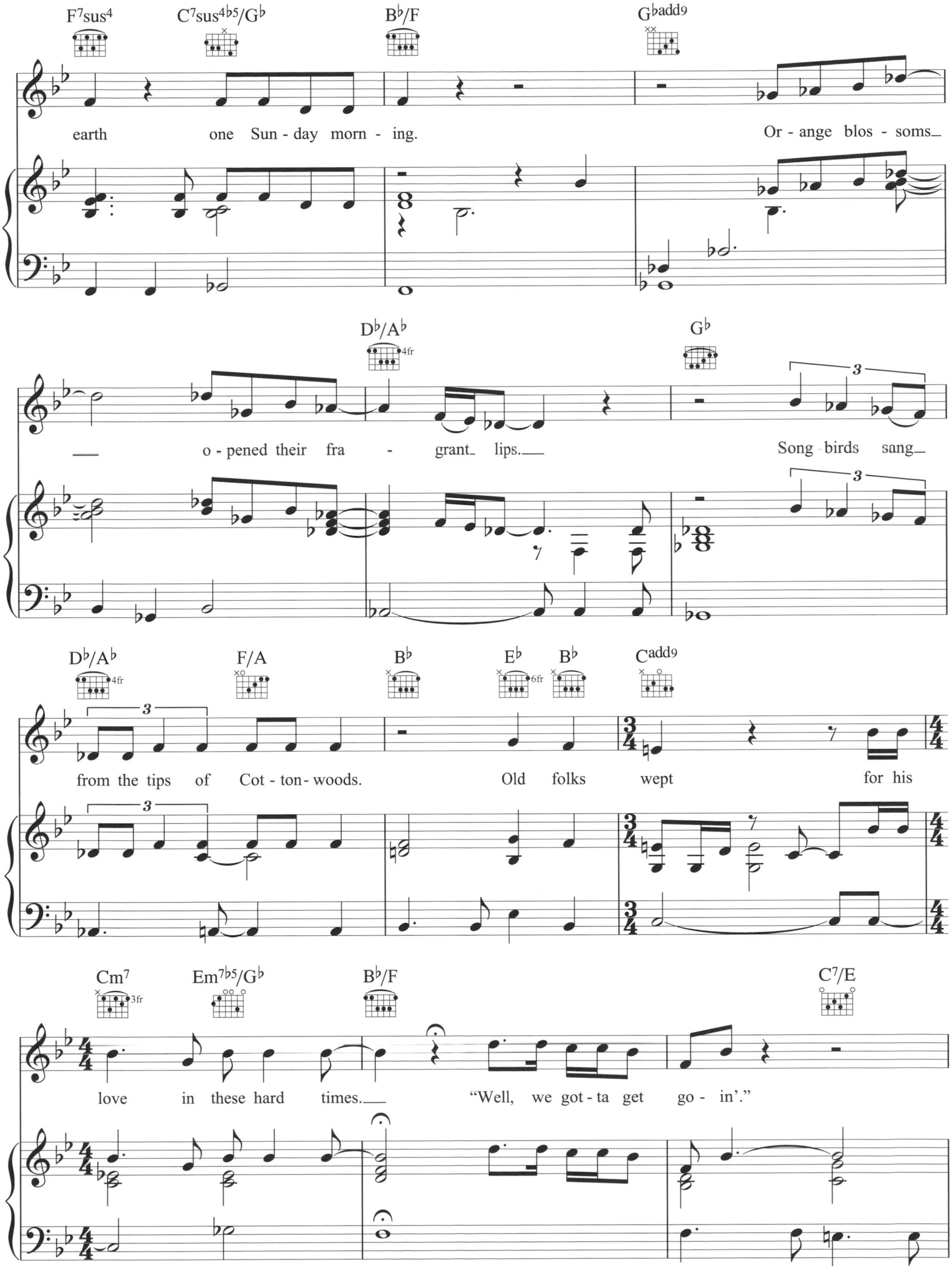
F7sus4 C7sus4♭5/G♭ B♭/F G♭add9
earth one Sun-day morn-ing. Or-ange blos-soms
D♭/A♭ G♭
opened their fra-grant lips. Song birds sang
D♭/A♭ F/A B♭ E♭ B♭ Cadd9
from the tips of Cot-ton-woods. Old folks wept for his
Cm7 Em7♭5/G♭ B♭/F C7/E
love in these hard times. "Well, we got-ta get go-in'."

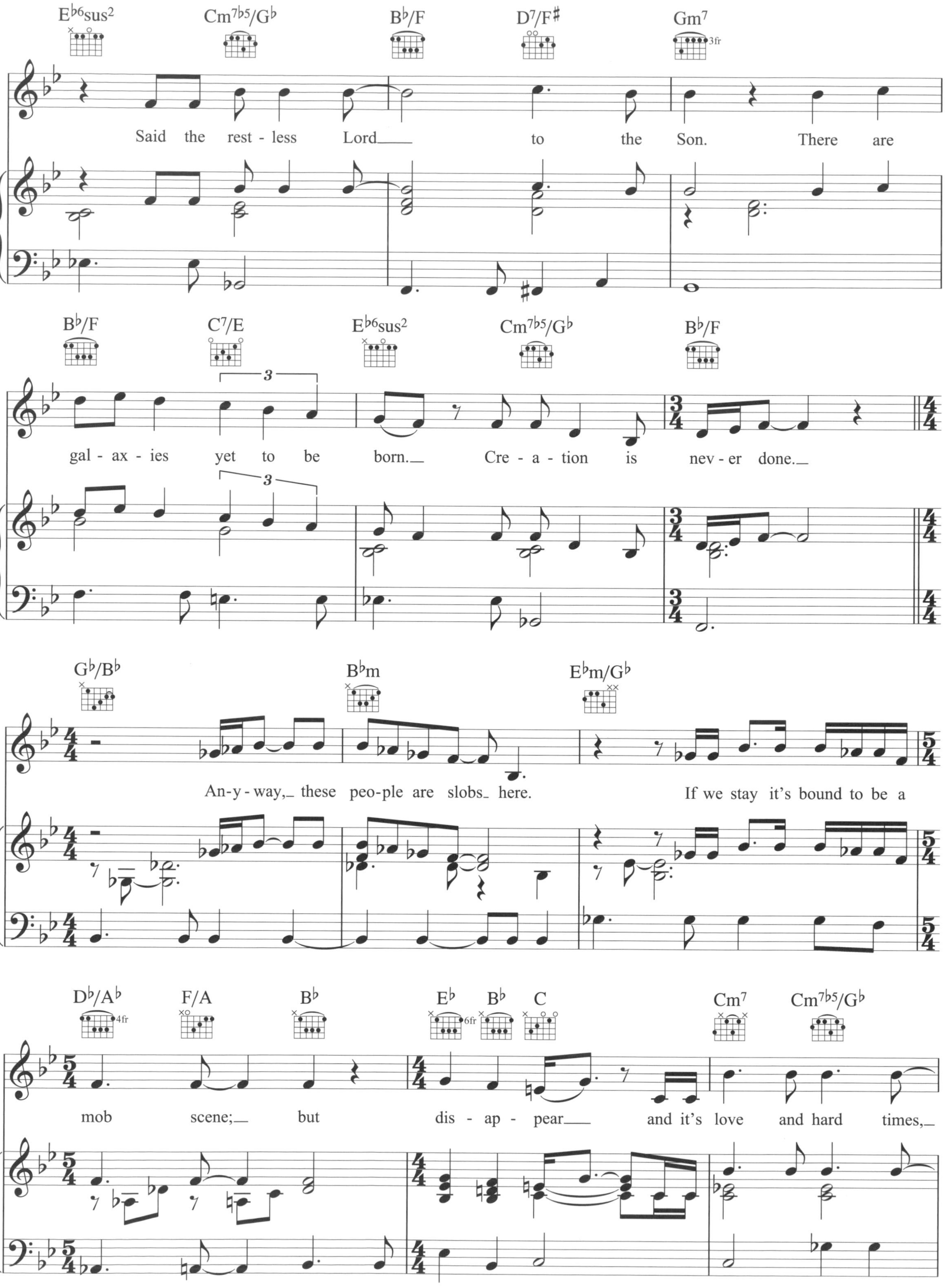
E♭6sus2 Cm7♭5/G♭ B♭/F D7/F♯ Gm7
Said the rest - less Lord to the Son. There are
B♭/F C7/E E♭6sus2 Cm7♭5/G♭ B♭/F
gal - ax - ies yet to be born. Cre - a - tion is nev - er done.
G♭/B♭ B♭m E♭m/G♭
An - y - way, these peo - ple are slobs here. If we stay it's bound to be a
D♭/A♭ F/A B♭ E♭ B♭ C Cm7 Cm7♭5/G♭
mob scene; but dis - ap - pear and it's love and hard times,

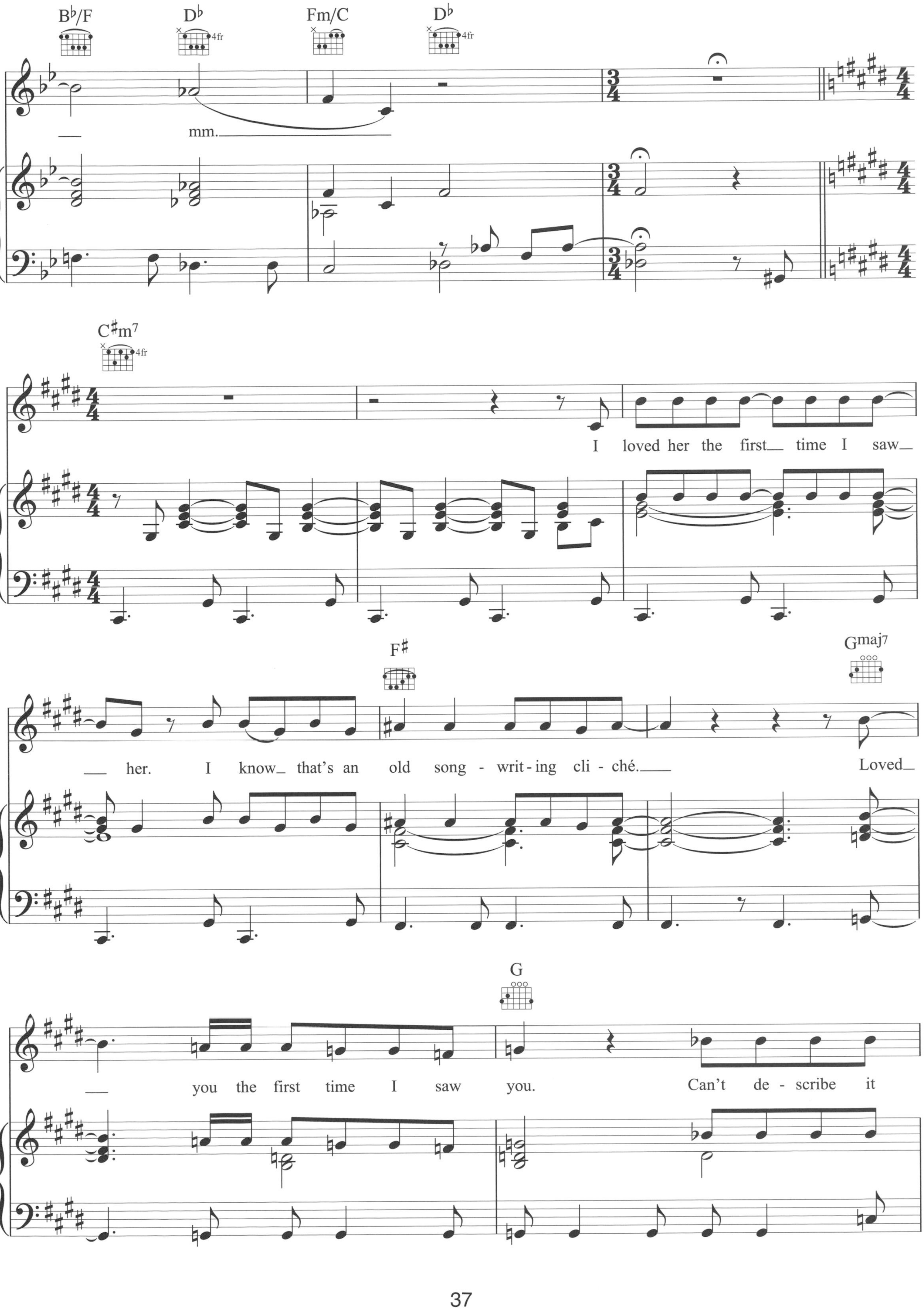
B♭/F
D♭
4fr
Fm/C
D♭
4fr
mm.
C♯m7
4fr
I loved her the first time I saw
her. I know that's an old song - writ - ing cli - ché.
F♯
Gmaj7
Loved
you the first time I saw you.
G
Can't de - scribe it

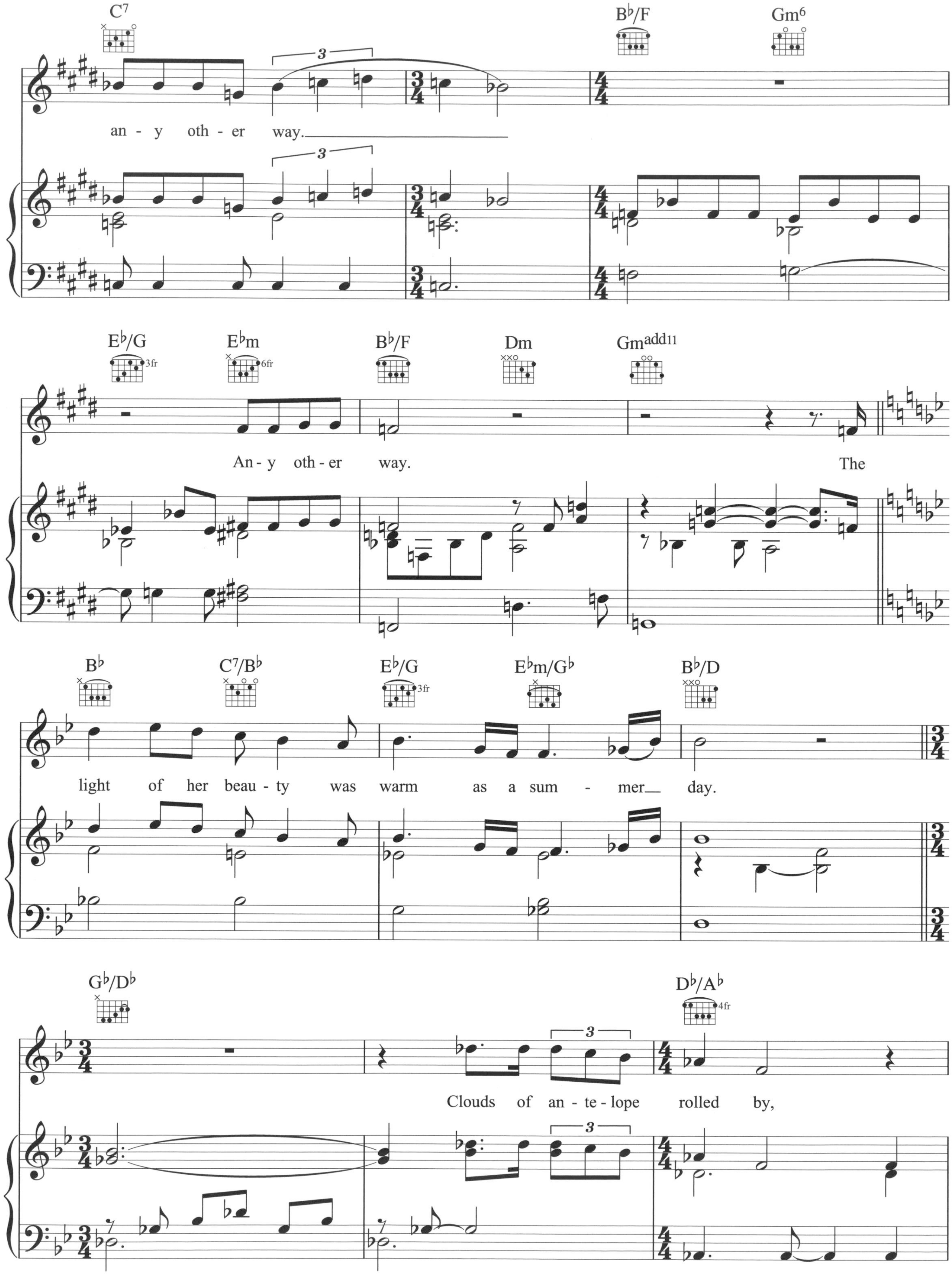
C7
B♭/F
Gm6
an - y oth - er way.
3
E♭/G
E♭m
B♭/F
Dm
Gmadd11
3fr
6fr
An - y oth - er way.
The
B♭
C7/B♭
E♭/G
E♭m/G♭
B♭/D
light of her beau - ty was warm as a sum - mer day.
G♭/D♭
D♭/A♭
4fr
Clouds of an - te - lope rolled by,

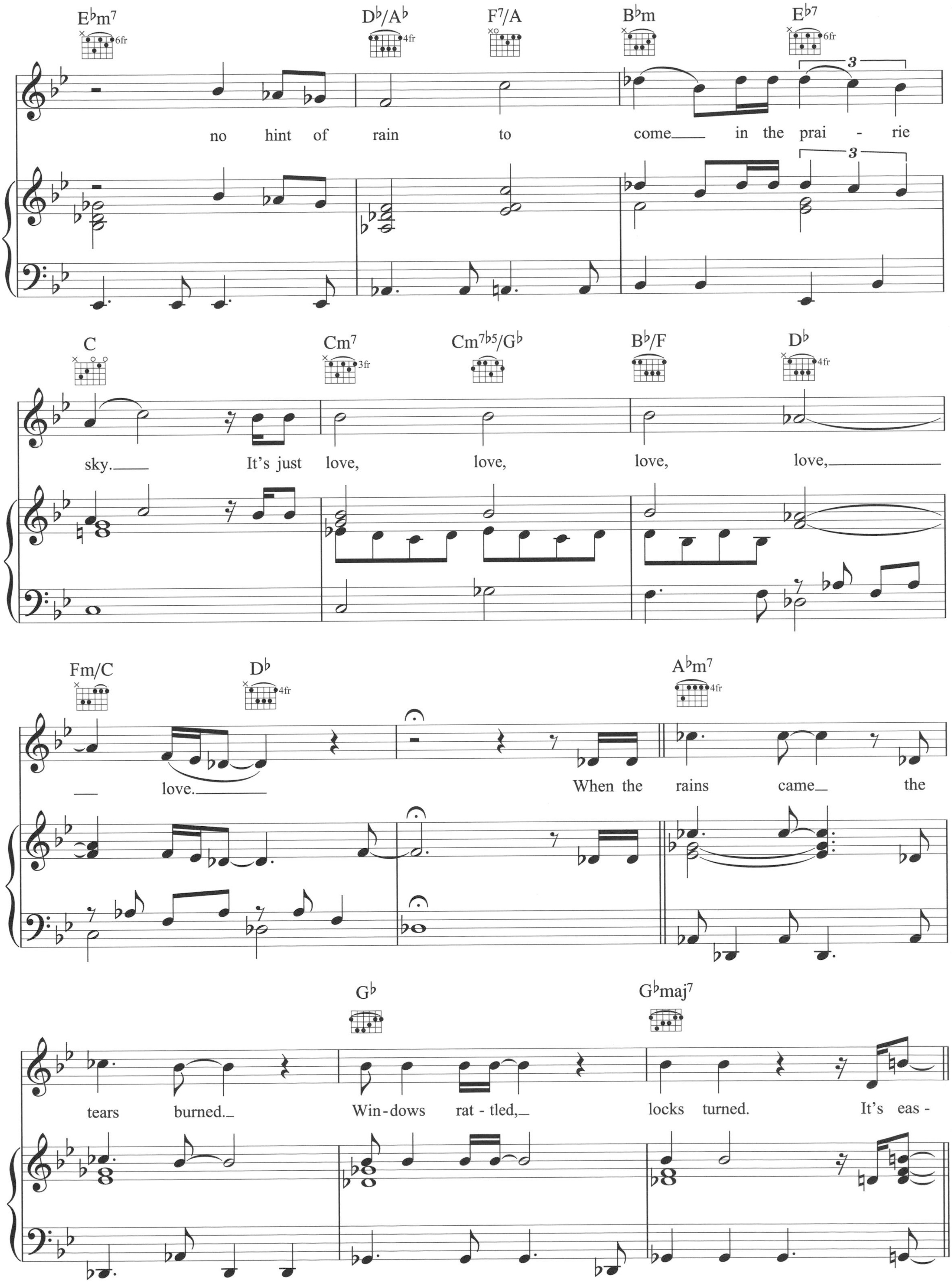
E♭m7
D♭/A♭
F7/A
B♭m
E♭7
no hint of rain to come in the prai - rie
C
Cm7
Cm7♭5/G♭
B♭/F
D♭
sky. It's just love, love, love, love,
Fm/C
D♭
A♭m7
love. When the rains came the
G♭
G♭maj7
tears burned. Win-dows rat - tled, locks turned. It's eas -

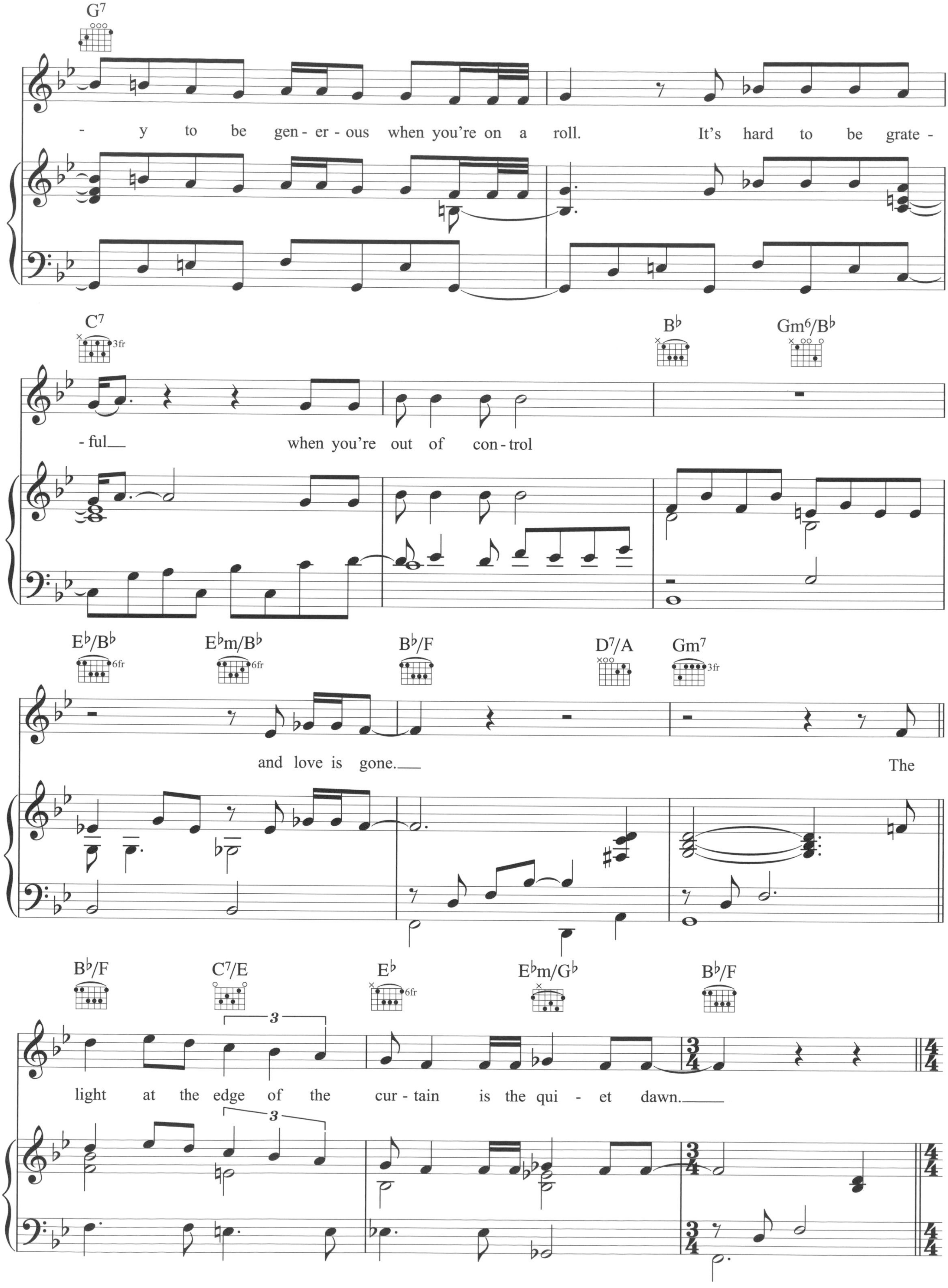
G7
- y to be gen - er - ous when you're on a roll. It's hard to be grate -
C7
Bb
Gm6/Bb
- ful when you're out of con - trol
Eb/Bb
Ebm/Bb
Bb/F
D7/A
Gm7
and love is gone. The
Bb/F
C7/E
Eb
Ebm/Gb
Bb/F
3
light at the edge of the cur - tain is the qui - et dawn.

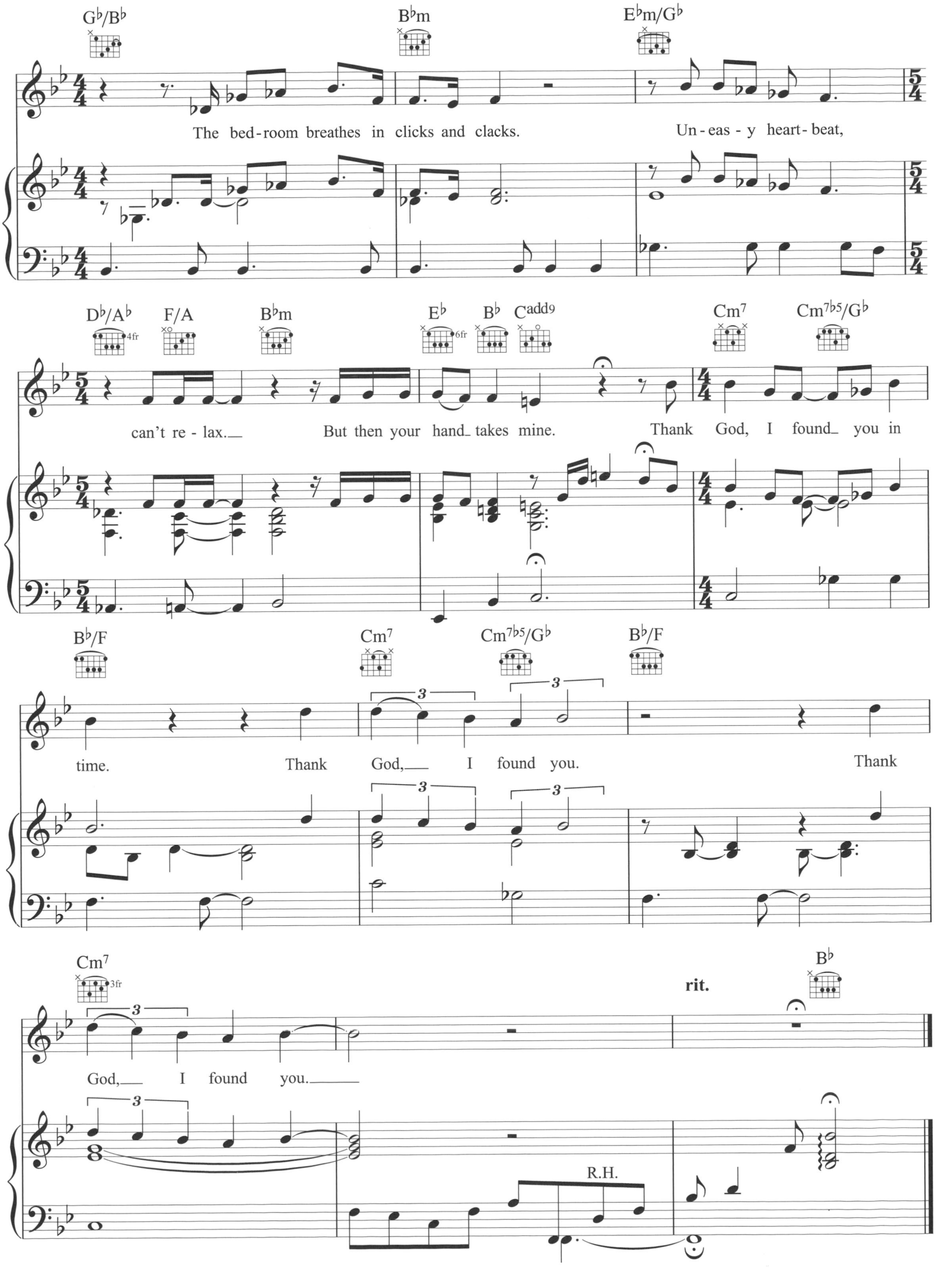
G♭/B♭
B♭m
E♭m/G♭
The bed-room breathes in clicks and clacks.
Un-eas-y heart-beat,
D♭/A♭
F/A
B♭m
E♭
B♭
Cadd9
Cm7
Cm7♭5/G♭
can't re-lax.
But then your hand takes mine.
Thank God, I found you in
B♭/F
Cm7
Cm7♭5/G♭
B♭/F
time.
Thank God, I found you.
Thank
Cm7
rit.
B♭
God, I found you.
R.H.

Love Is Eternal Sacred Light

Words & Music by Paul Simon

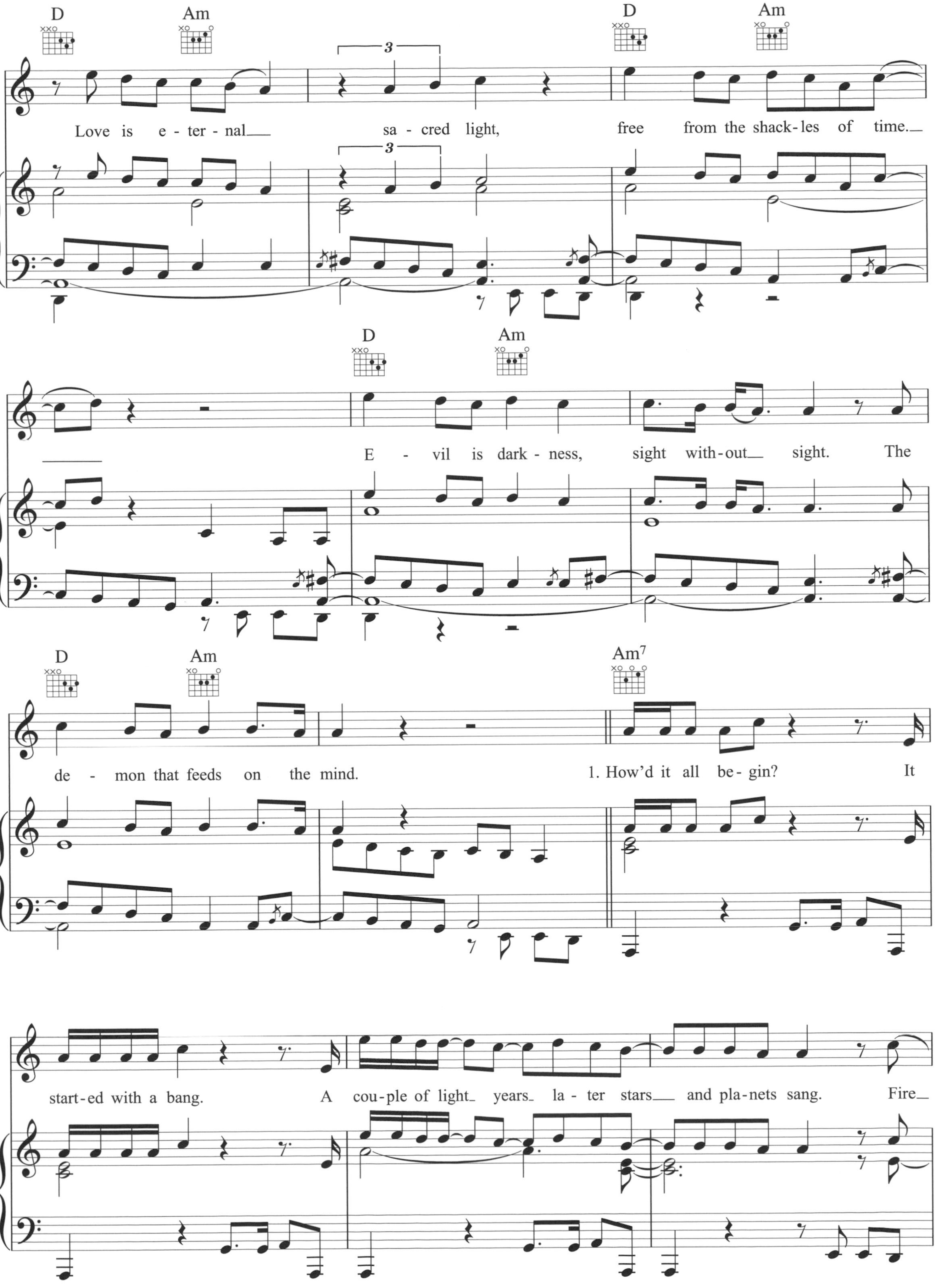
D Am D Am
3
Love is e - ter - nal sa - cred light, free from the shack - les of time.
D Am
E - vil is dark - ness, sight with - out sight. The
D Am Am7
de - mon that feeds on the mind. 1. How'd it all be - gin? It
start - ed with a bang. A cou - ple of light years la - ter stars and pla - nets sang. Fire

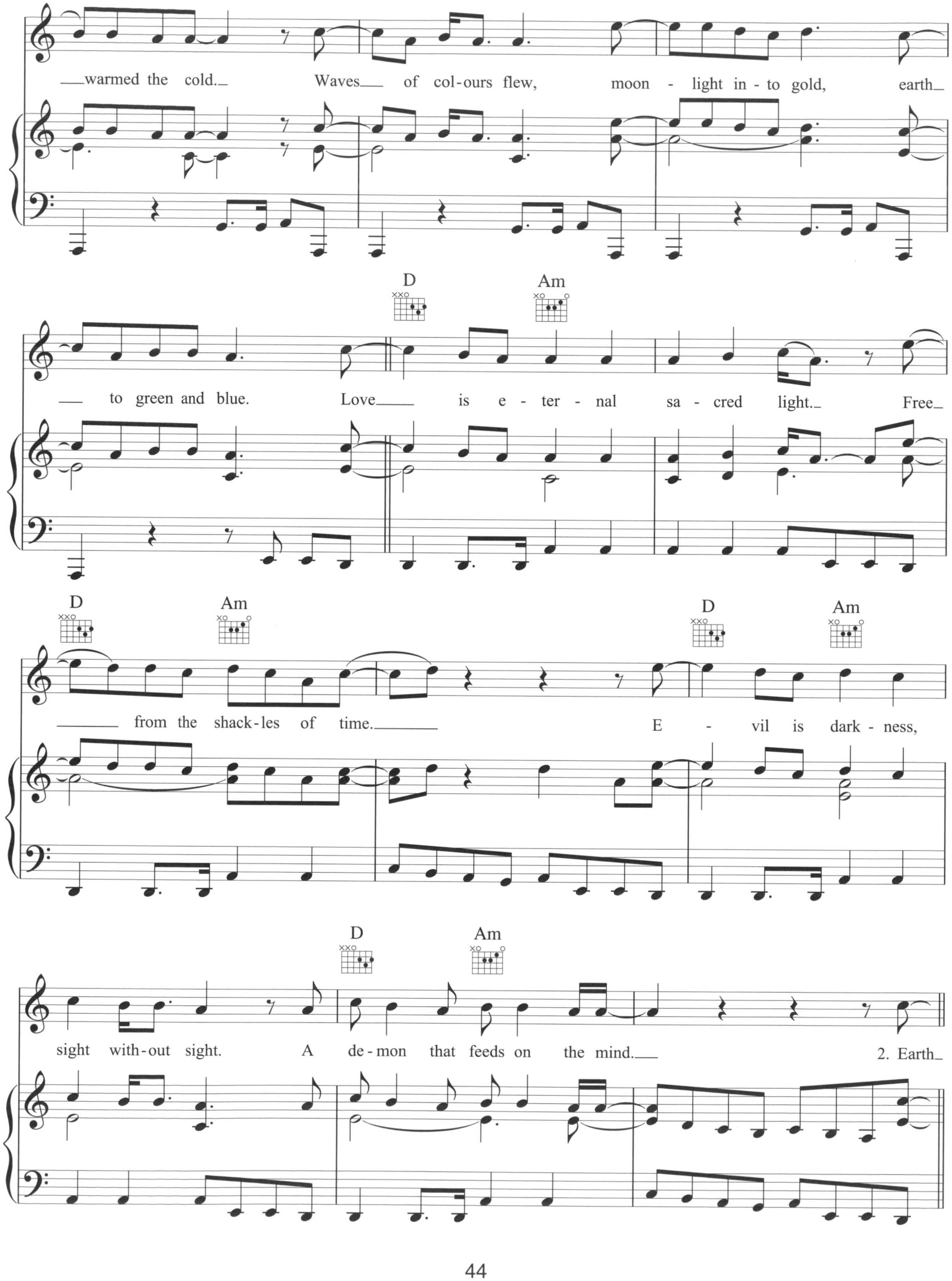

warmed the cold. Waves of col-ours flew, moon - light in - to gold, earth
D
Am
to green and blue. Love is e - ter - nal sa - cred light. Free
D
Am
D
Am
from the shack-les of time. E - vil is dark - ness,
D
Am
sight with-out sight. A de - mon that feeds on the mind. 2. Earth

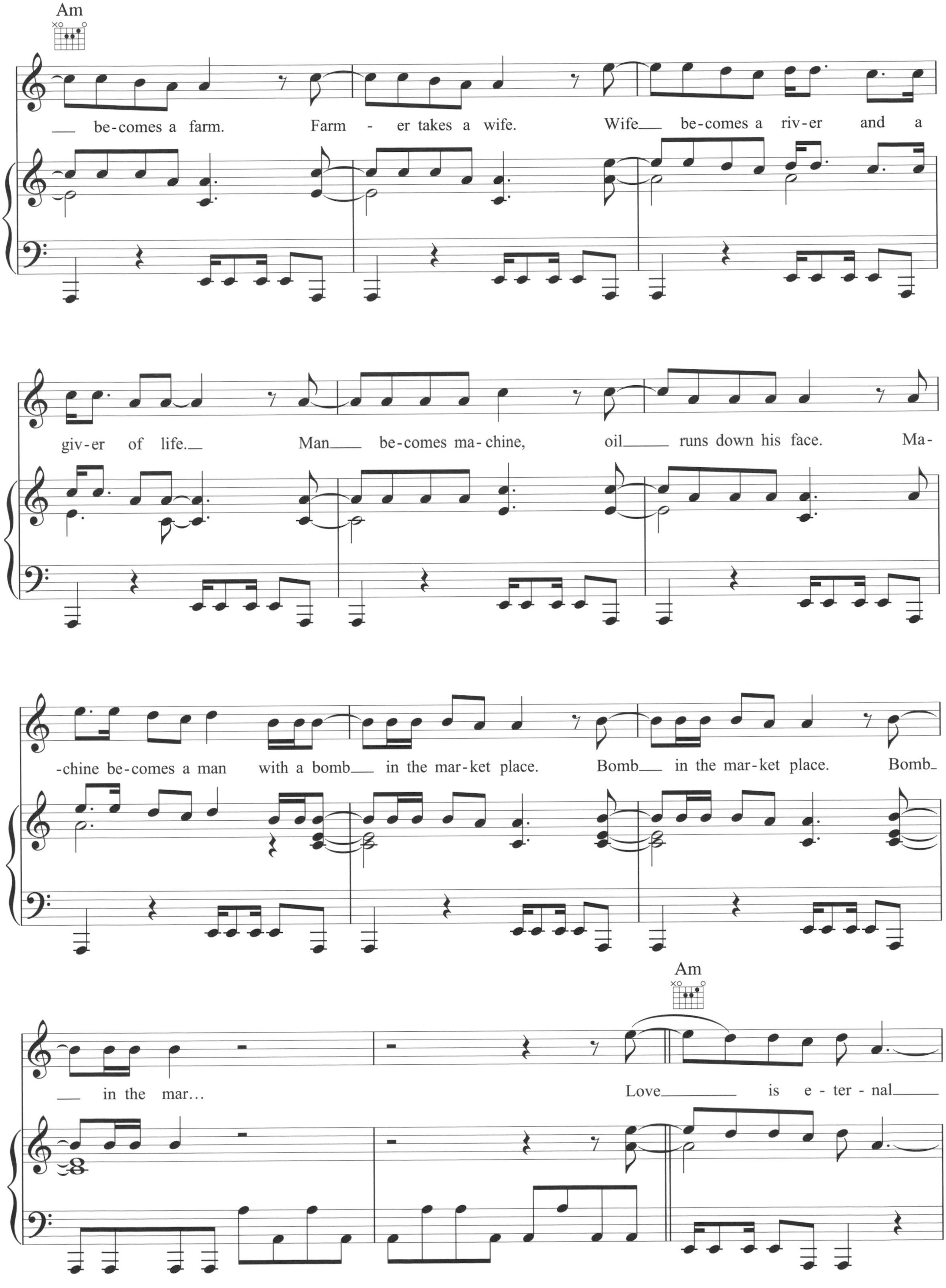
Am
be-comes a farm. Farm - er takes a wife. Wife be-comes a riv-er and a
giv-er of life. Man be-comes ma-chine, oil runs down his face. Ma-
-chine be-comes a man with a bomb in the mar-ket place. Bomb in the mar-ket place. Bomb
in the mar…
Am
Love is e-ter-nal

— sa - cred light, free from the shack-les of time. E -
- vil is dark - ness, sight with-out sight. A de - mon that feeds on the mind.
Am
(Harmonica solo)
A5/E
8vb

N.C.
8vb till *
Big bang, that's a joke that I made up once when I had e-ons to kill.
me, love me, that's the main re-quest I re-ceive.
Drums
You know most folks, they don't get when I'm jok-ing well,
Well, you know I love all of my child-ren and it
1.
2.
may-be some day they will. Love
tears me up when I leave.
* But
3
G
some-times you got-ta fly down that high-way,
check out the ra-di-o, pop mu-sic sta-tion.
end of the dial there's a gos-pel show. May-be

D
free as a bird. Knock on wood, thank the Lord I'm
That don't sound like my mu - sic to me.
now I can ex - it and rest. There's a
G
driv - ing a - long in my au - to - mo - bile. It's a
Talk - show host, what's that boys name?
bliz - zard rol - ling down off the banks of Lake Mi - chi - gan, gon -
1, 2.
D
3.
brand new, pre - owned nine-ty-six Ford.
Po - li - tics is ug - ly. And the
-na cov - er the roads of the
i - cy Mid - west.

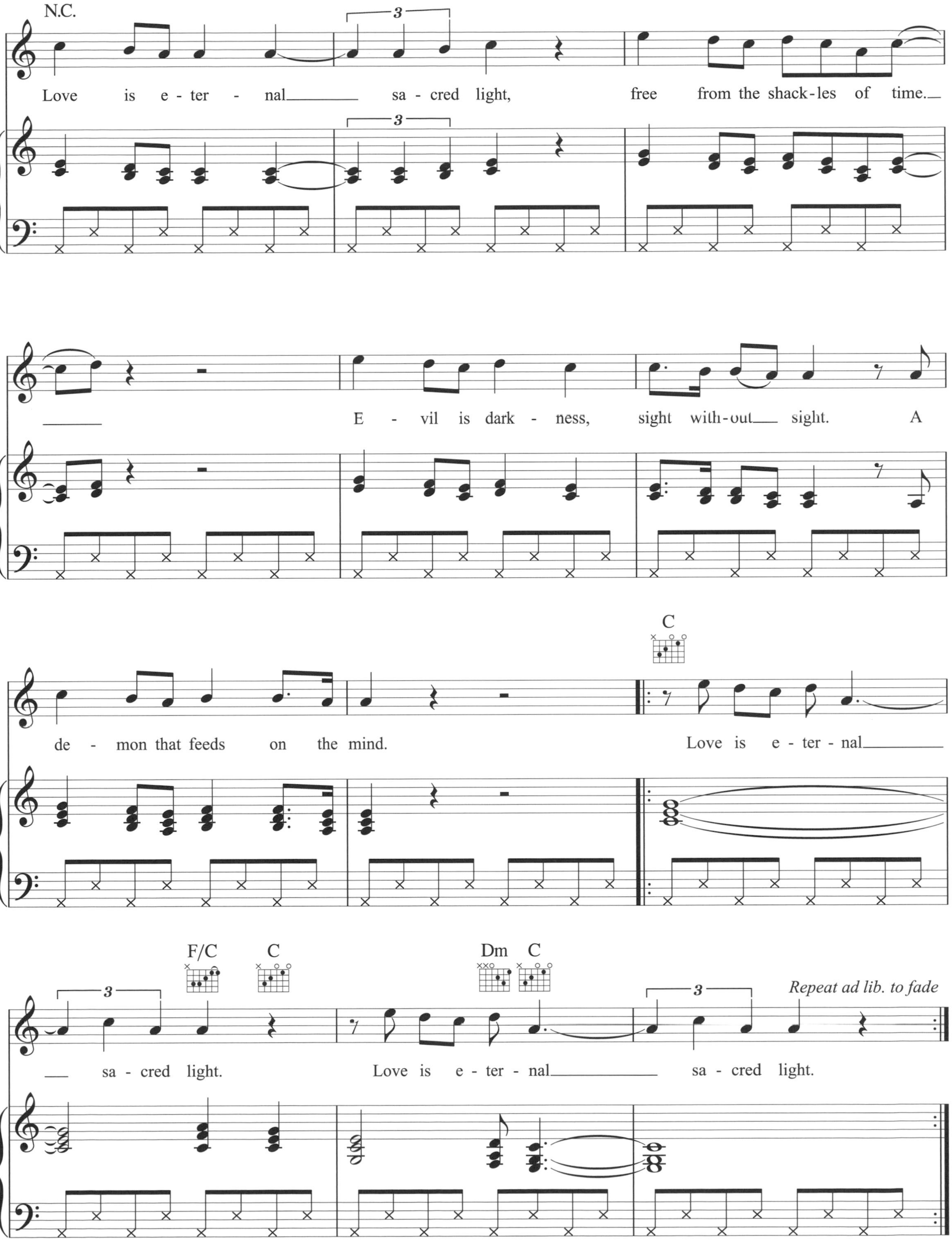
N.C.
Love is e-ter-nal sa-cred light, free from the shack-les of time.
E-vil is dark-ness, sight with-out sight. A de-mon that feeds on the mind.
C
Love is e-ter-nal
F/C C Dm C
sa-cred light. Love is e-ter-nal sa-cred light.
Repeat ad lib. to fade

Amulet

Music by Paul Simon

Questions for the Angels

Words & Music by Paul Simon

♩. = 46
Freely
Dmaj7add13
G6
Aadd9
Con pedale
Dmaj7add13
Dmaj7add13
1. A pil - grim on a pil - grim - age
(2.) shop for love in a bar - gain store and
G6
Aadd9
Dmaj7add13
walked a - cross the Brook - lyn Bridge, his sneak - ers torn. In the
you don't get what you bar - gained for, can you get your mon - ey back? If an

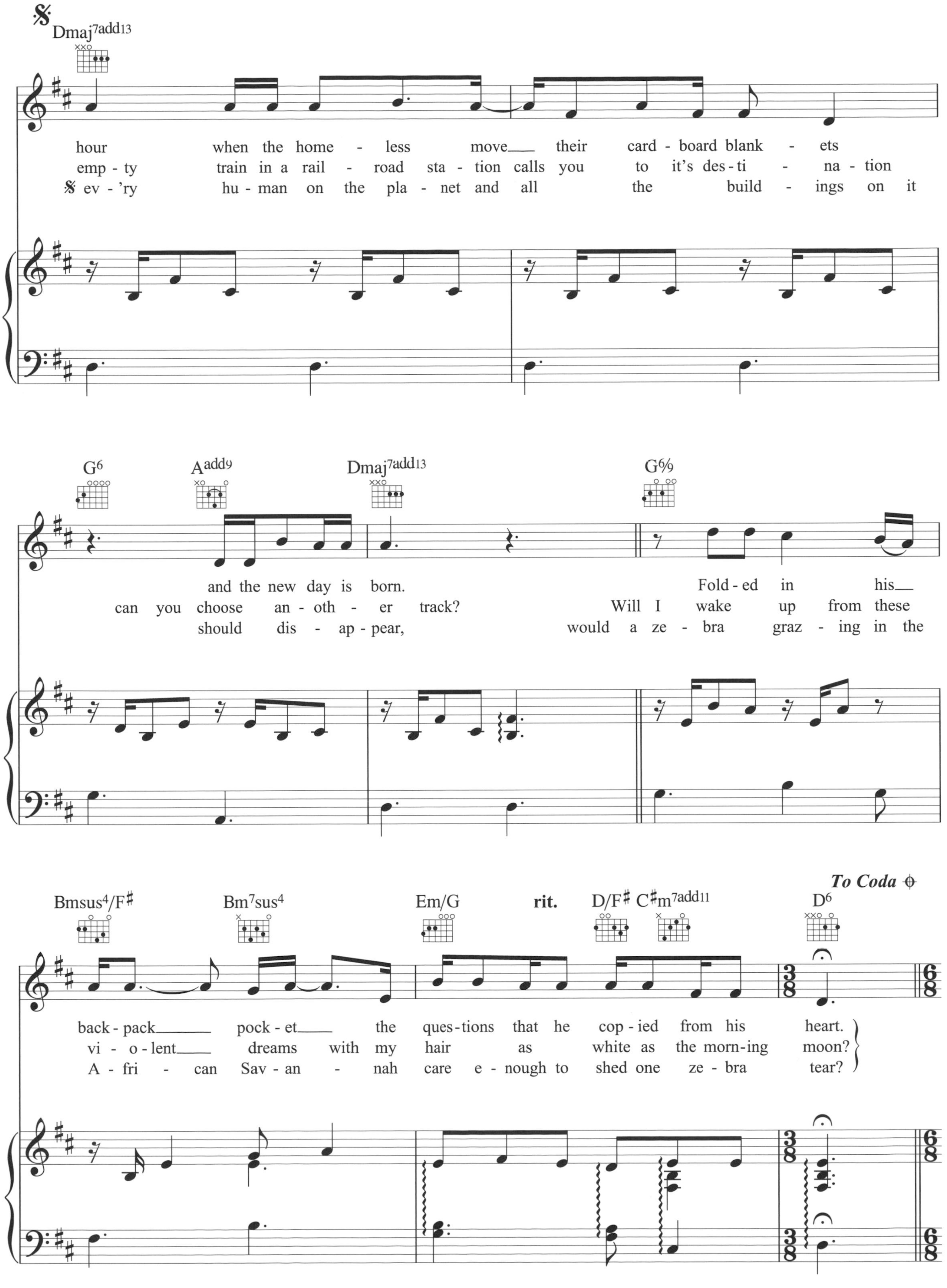
Dmaj7add13
hour when the home - less move their card - board blank - ets
emp - ty train in a rail - road sta - tion calls you to it's des - ti - na - tion
ev - 'ry hu - man on the pla - net and all the build - ings on it
G6
Aadd9
Dmaj7add13
G6/9
and the new day is born. Fold - ed in his
can you choose an - oth - er track? Will I wake up from these
should dis - ap - pear, would a ze - bra graz - ing in the
To Coda
Bmsus4/F♯
Bm7sus4
Em/G
rit.
D/F♯
C♯m7add11
D6
back - pack pock - et the ques - tions that he cop - ied from his heart.
vi - o - lent dreams with my hair as white as the morn - ing moon?
A - fri - can Sav - an - nah care e - nough to shed one ze - bra tear?

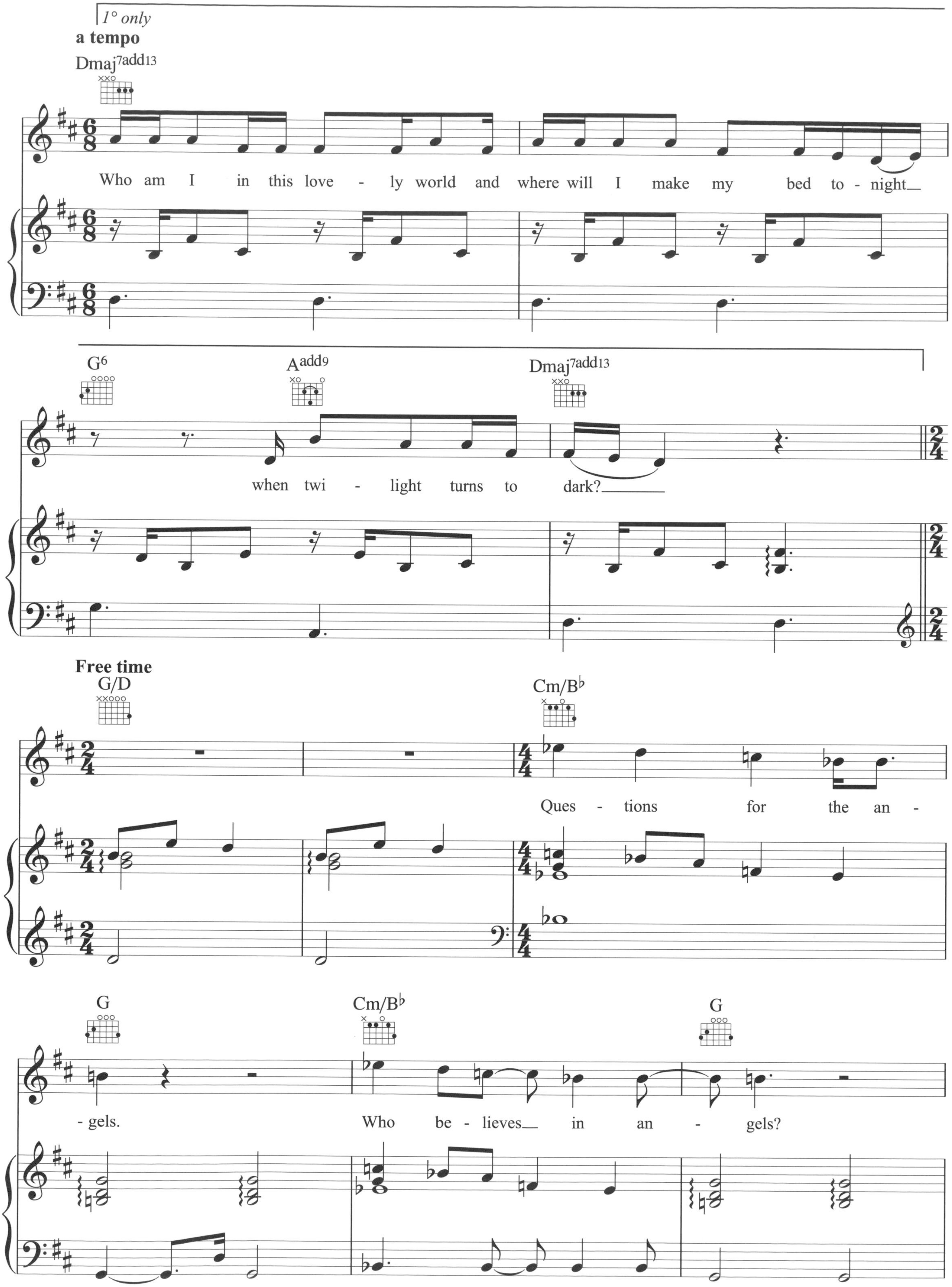
1° only
a tempo
Dmaj7add13
Who am I in this love - ly world and where will I make my bed to - night
G6
Aadd9
Dmaj7add13
when twi - light turns to dark?
Free time
G/D
Cm/B♭
Ques - tions for the an -
G
Cm/B♭
G
- gels. Who be - lieves in an - gels?

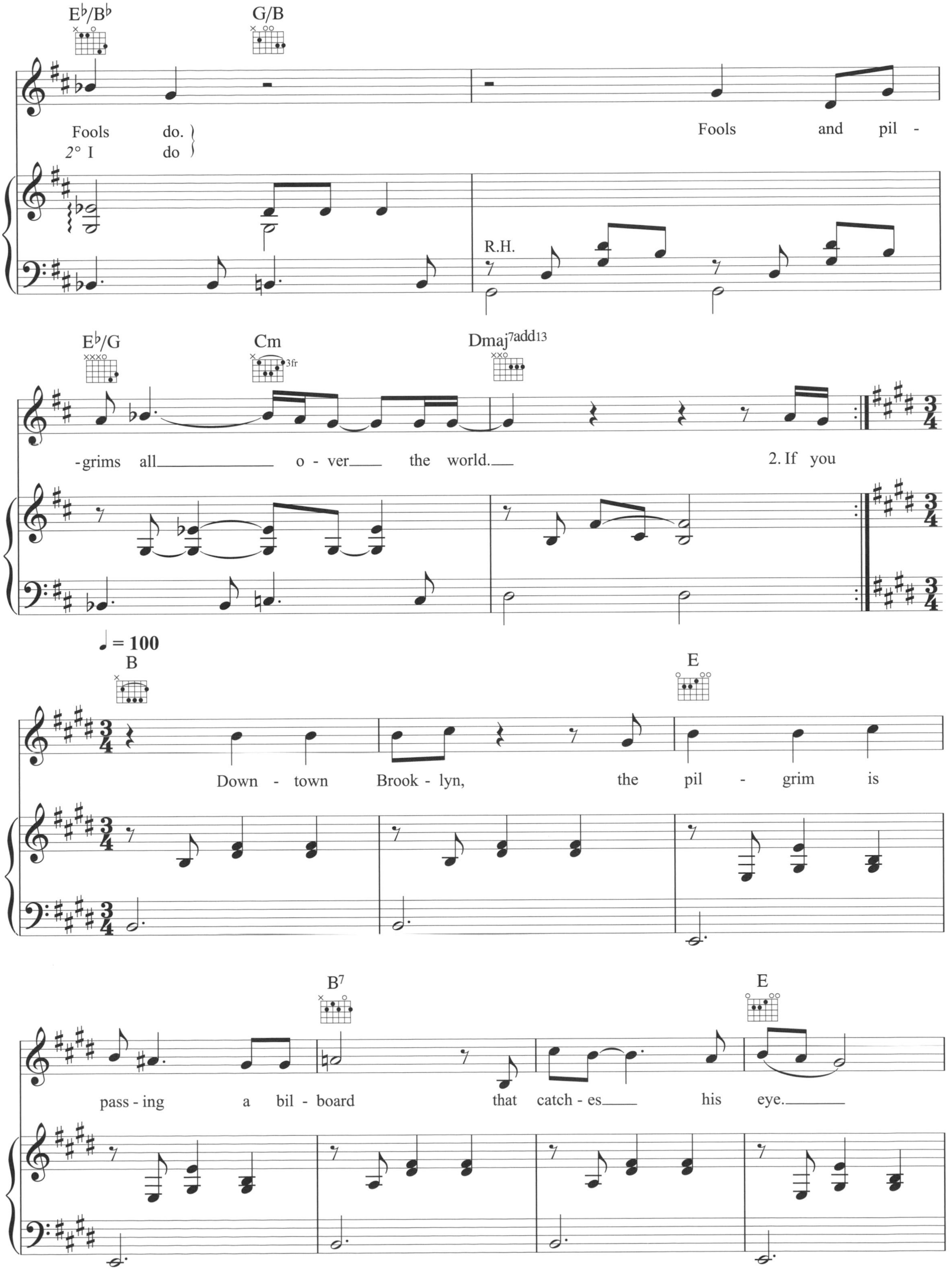
E♭/B♭
G/B
Fools do.
2° I do
Fools and pil-
R.H.
E♭/G
Cm
3fr
Dmaj7add13
-grims all over the world.
2. If you
♩ = 100
B
E
Down-town Brook-lyn, the pil-grim is
B7
E
pass-ing a bil-board that catch-es his eye.

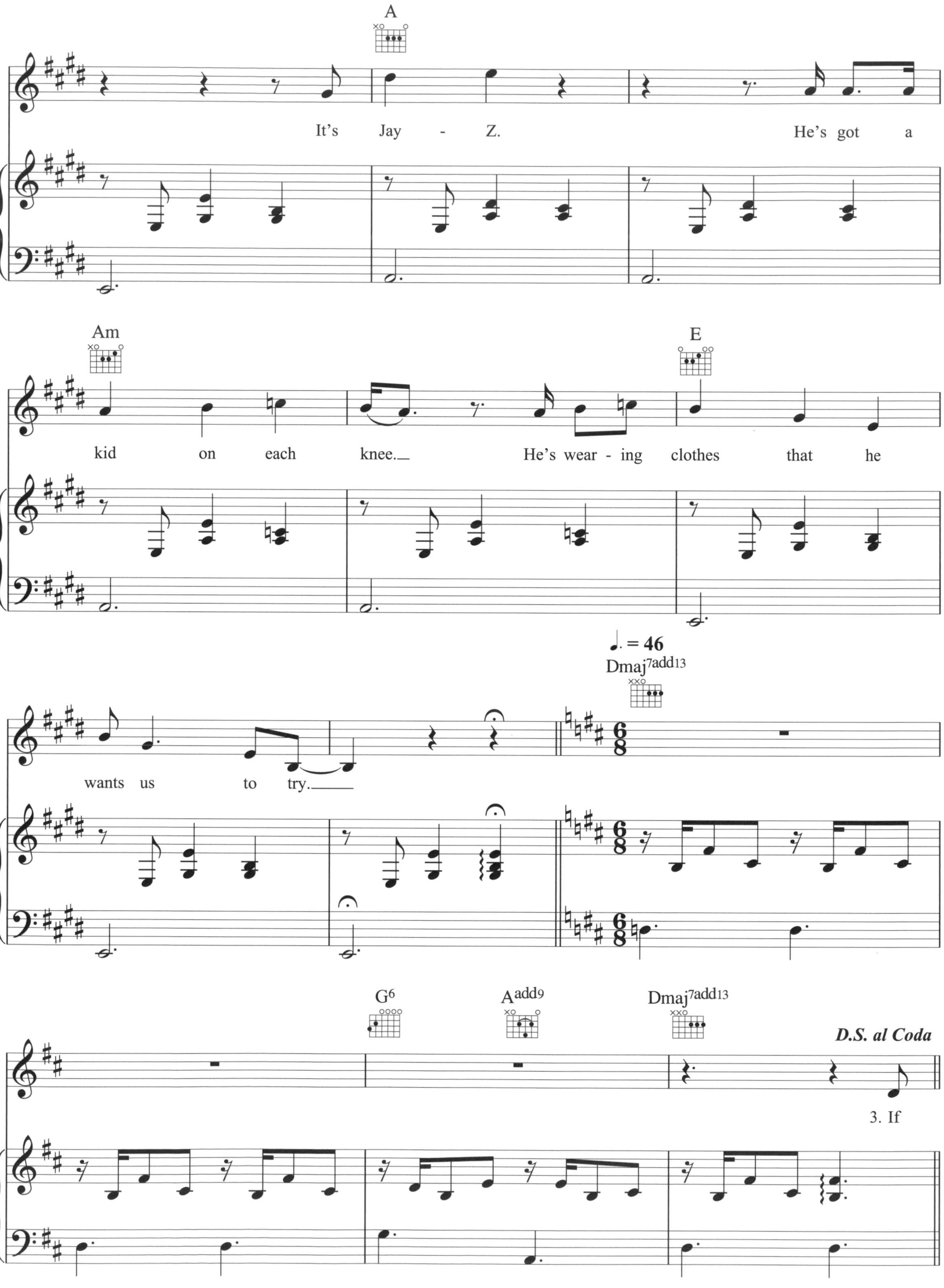

A
It's Jay - Z. He's got a
Am
E
kid on each knee. He's wear - ing clothes that he
wants us to try.
♩. = 46
Dmaj7add13
G6
Aadd9
Dmaj7add13
D.S. al Coda
3. If

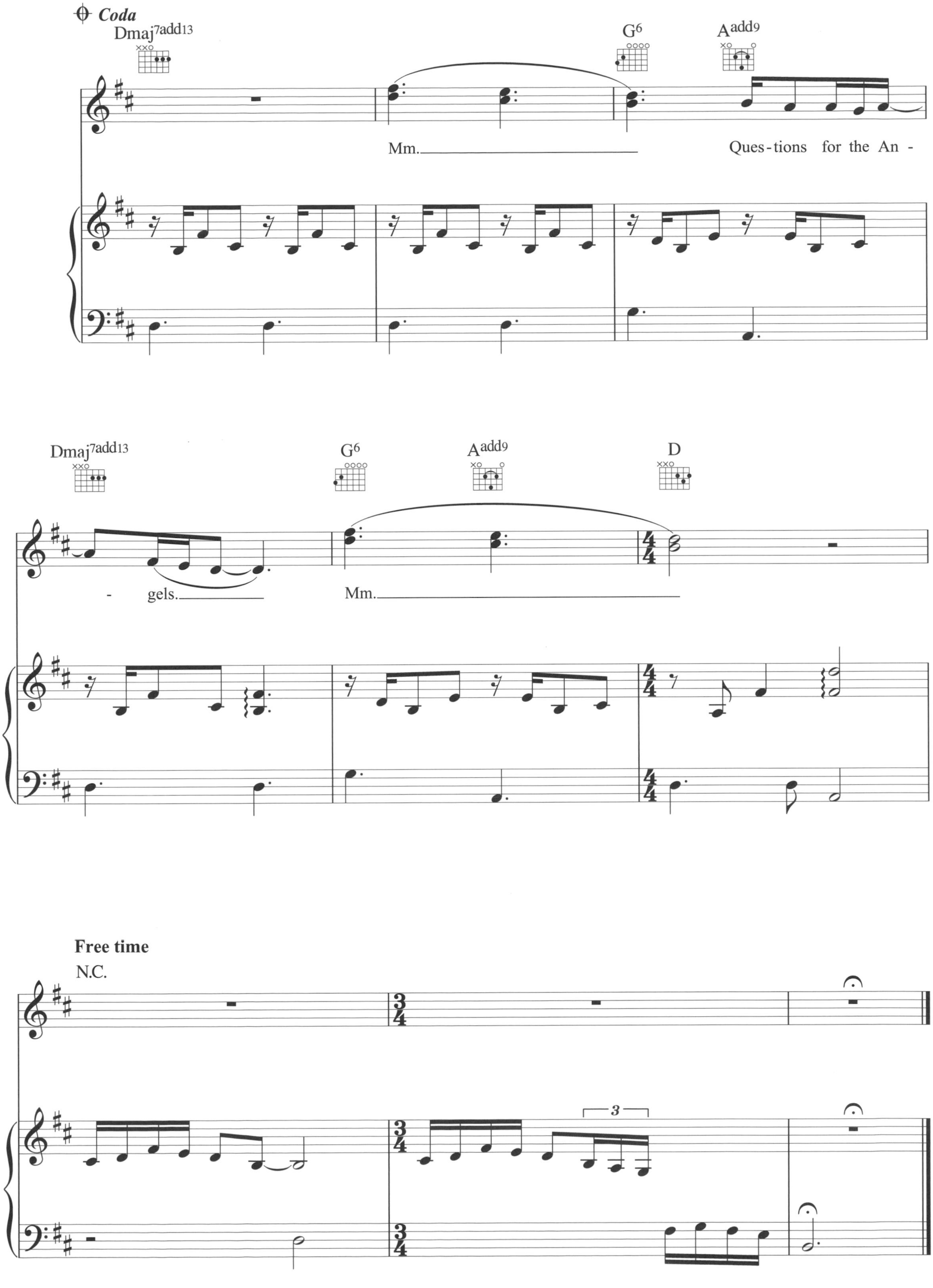
Coda
Dmaj7add13
G6
Aadd9
Mm.
Ques-tions for the An -
Dmaj7add13
G6
Aadd9
D
- gels.
Mm.
Free time
N.C.
3

Love & Blessings

Words & Music by Paul Simon

Em
1. Love and bless - ings, sim - ple kind - ness
2. If the sum - mer kept a se - cret
fell like rain on the thirst - y land.
it was heav - en's lack of rain.

Fields and gar - dens long a - ban - doned
Gold - en days and am - ber sun - sets.
D/F♯
came to life in dust and sand.
Let the sci - en - tist com - plain.
Em/G
Lov - er's lips, sweet as hon - ey
Came the Au - tumn, drained of col - our.
touched as if old love was new.
Ghosts in the wa - ter begged for more.

Ban - ker's pock - ets o - ver flow - ing with gold and mon - ey.
Ma - ple tears, just a lit - tle bit dull - er than the
To Coda
Pro - phe - cies of wealth come true.
mem - 'ry of the year be - fore.
N.C.
3
(Bop - bop a - whoa.)
Ain't no song like an old song, Char - lie.
8vb
Drums
(Bop - bop a - whoa.)
There ain't no song like an old song, Char - lie.

(Bop-bop a-whoa.) There ain't no time like a good time, Charlie,
8vb
bop-bop a-whoa. Ain't no times like the good times, Char-lie,
8vb
N.C.
Bop-bop a-whoa, whoa. The bop-bop a-whoa, the
cont. sim.
bop-bop a-whoa. Ev-'ry-where you look, an-y-where you go, ev-'ry-bod-y work-ing for the...

(Bop-bop a- whoa.) The bop-bop a-whoa, the bop-bop a-whoa. Can't get e-nough of that
3
bop-bop a-whoa, bop-bop a-whoa. (Bop-bop a-whoa.)
Em
D.S. al Coda

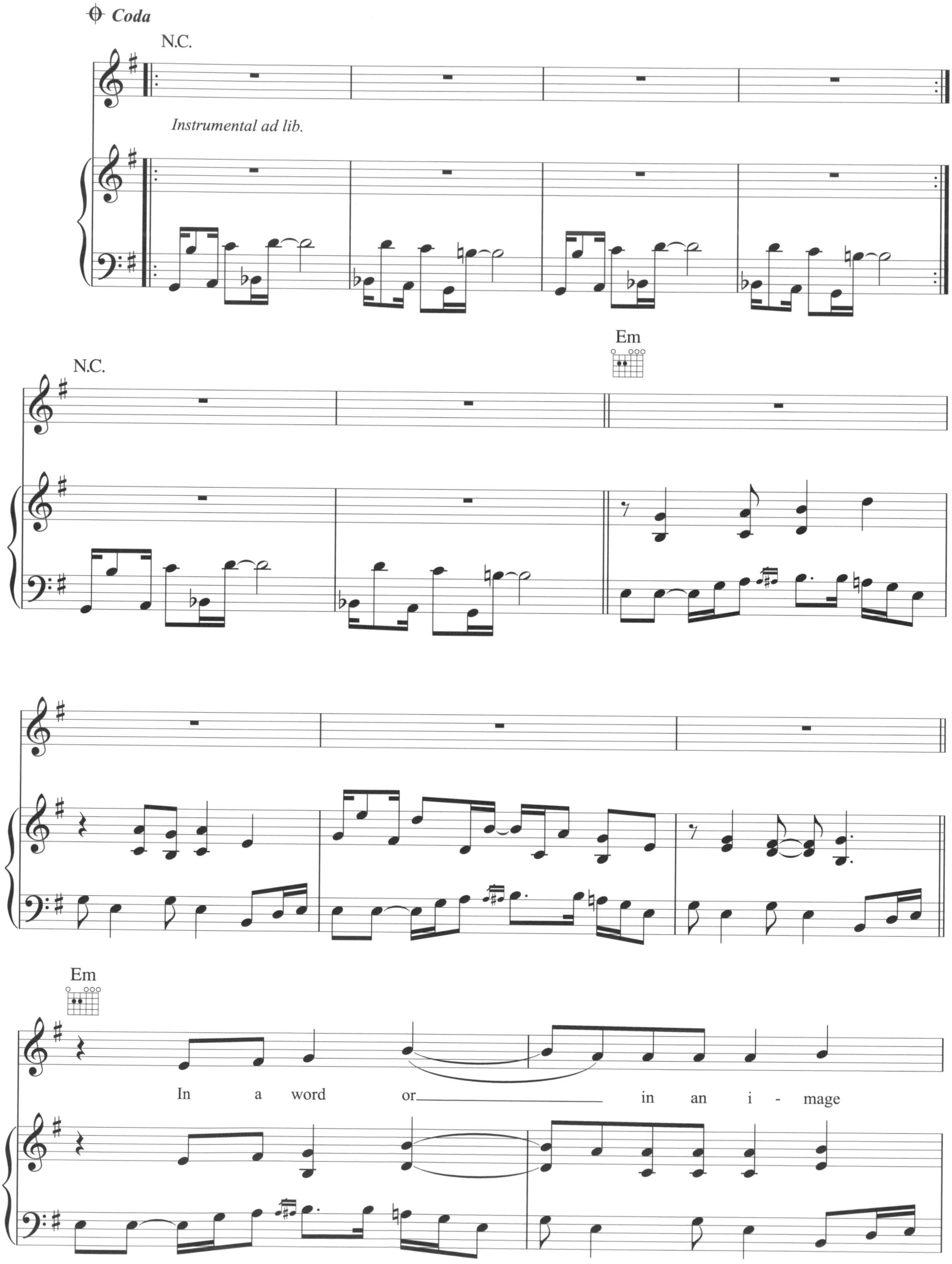
Coda
N.C.
Instrumental ad lib.
N.C.
Em
Em
In a word or in an i - mage

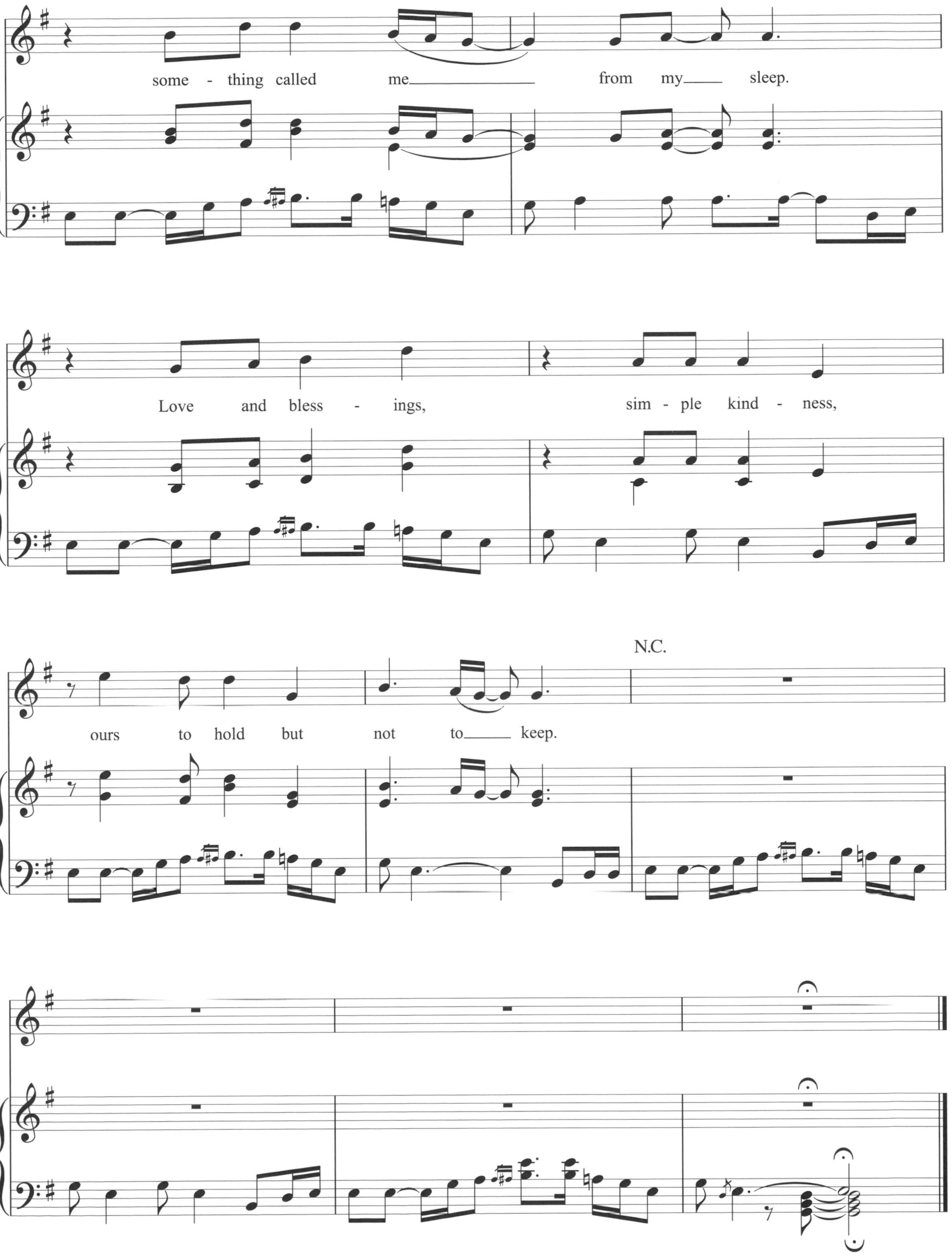
some - thing called me from my sleep.
Love and bless - ings, sim - ple kind - ness,
N.C.
ours to hold but not to keep.

So Beautiful or So What

Words & Music by Paul Simon

I'm gon-na fla-vour it with ok - ra,
Will it have a hap-py end - ing?
cay - enne pep-per to make it hot.
May - be yeah, and may-be not.
You know
I tell them
life is what we make of it, so beau-ti-ful or so what.
life is what we make of it, so beau-ti-ful or so what.
1.
2. I'm gon - na

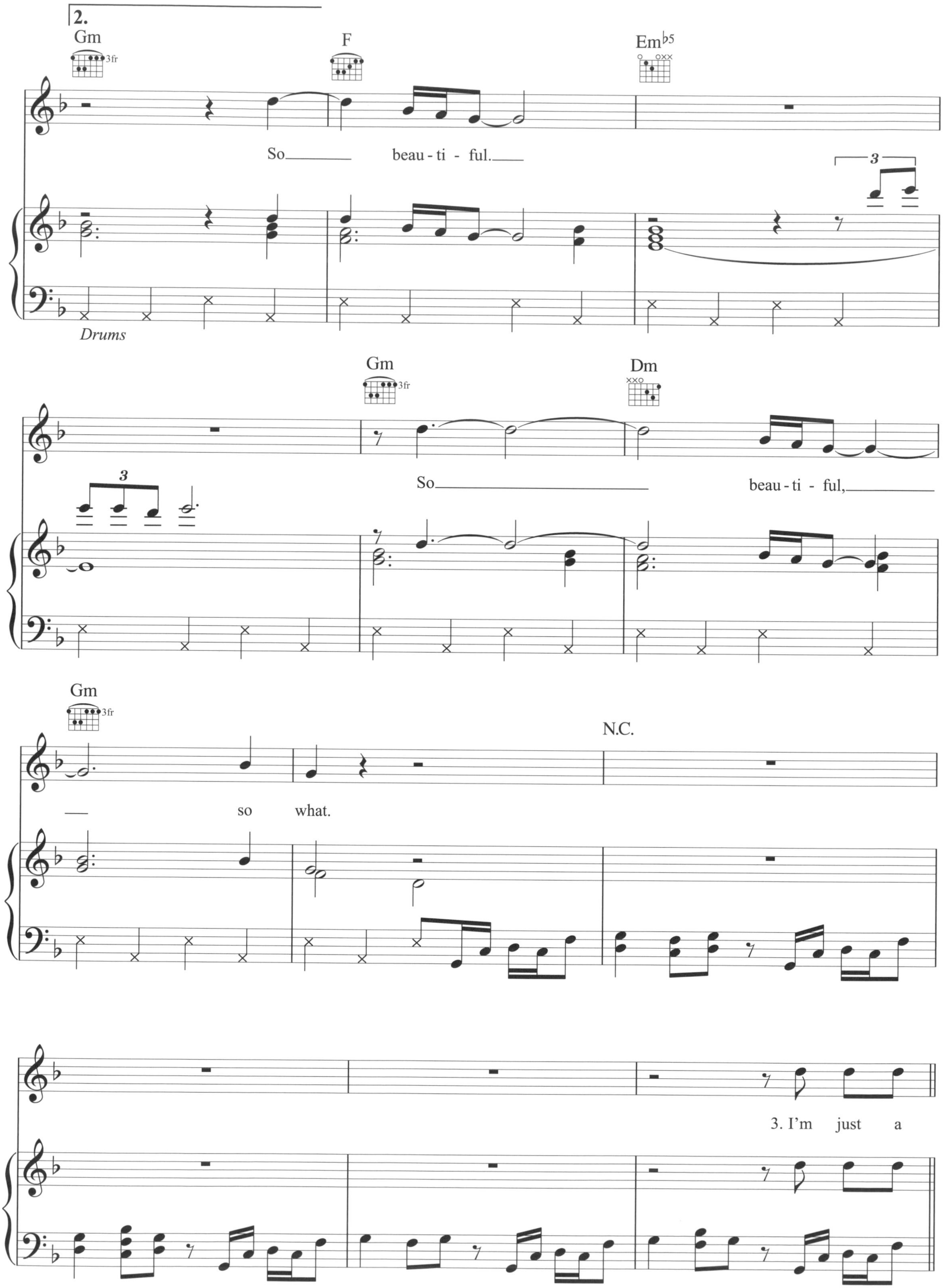
2.
Gm
3fr
F
Em♭5
So
beau - ti - ful.
3
Drums
Gm
3fr
Dm
3
So
beau - ti - ful,
Gm
3fr
N.C.
so
what.
3. I'm
just
a

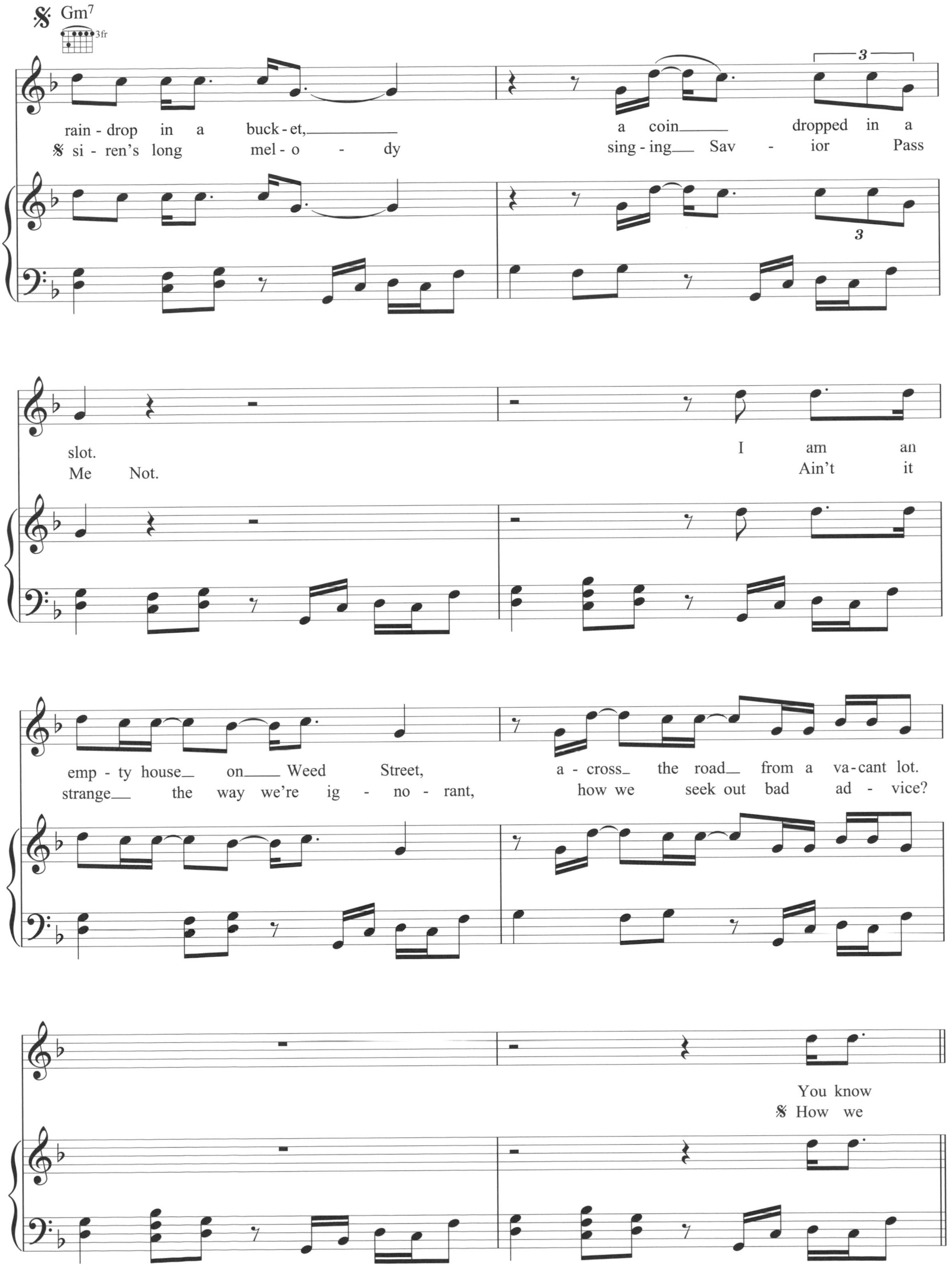
Gm7
3fr
rain - drop in a buck - et, a coin dropped in a
si - ren's long mel - o - dy sing - ing Sav - ior Pass
slot. I am an
Me Not. Ain't it
emp - ty house on Weed Street, a - cross the road from a va - cant lot.
strange the way we're ig - no - rant, how we seek out bad ad - vice?
You know
How we

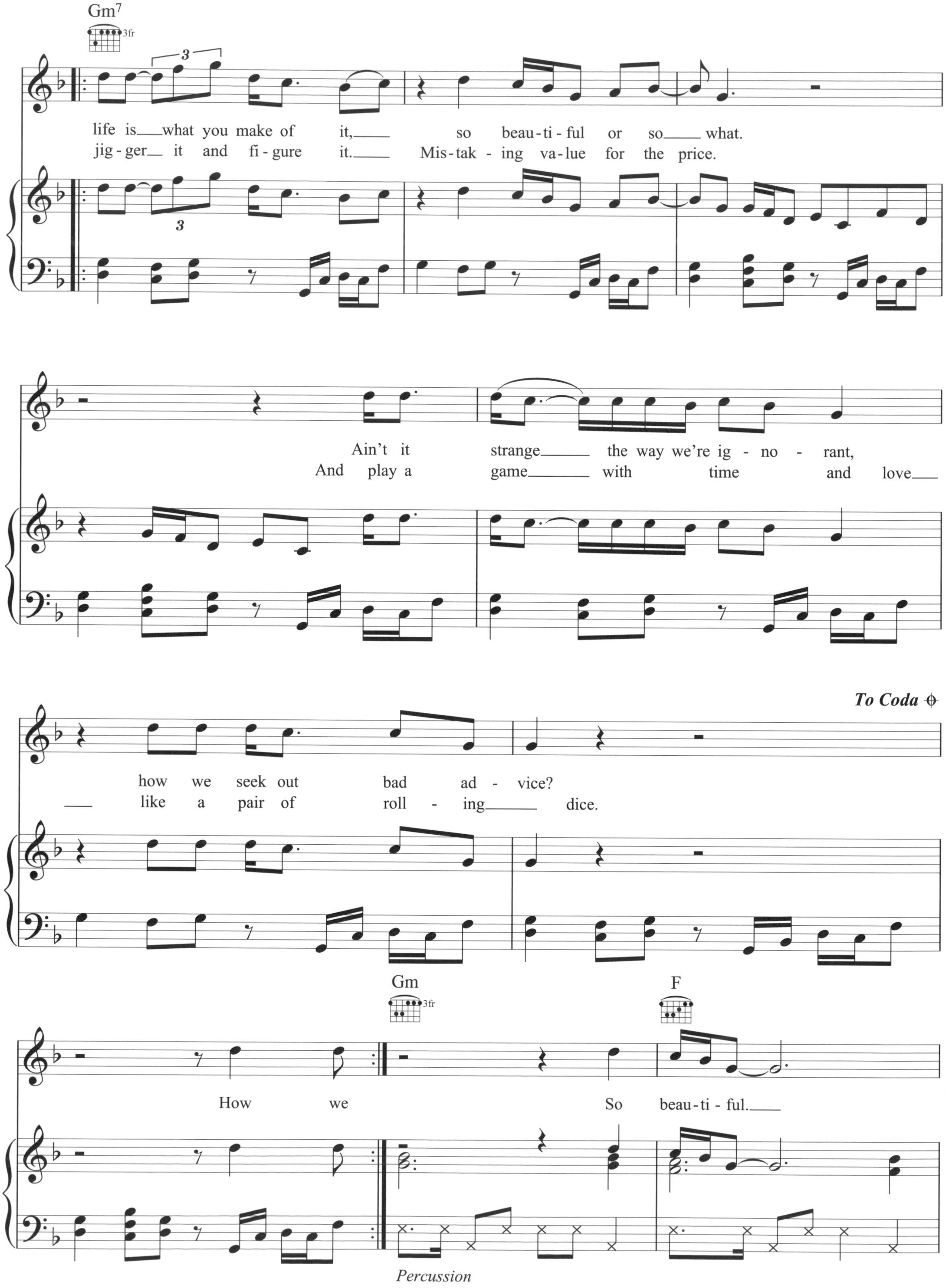
Gm7
3fr
3
life is what you make of it, so beau-ti-ful or so what.
jig-ger it and fi-gure it. Mis-tak-ing va-lue for the price.
3
Ain't it strange the way we're ig-no-rant,
And play a game with time and love
To Coda
how we seek out bad ad-vice?
like a pair of roll-ing dice.
Gm
3fr
F
How we So beau-ti-ful.
Percussion

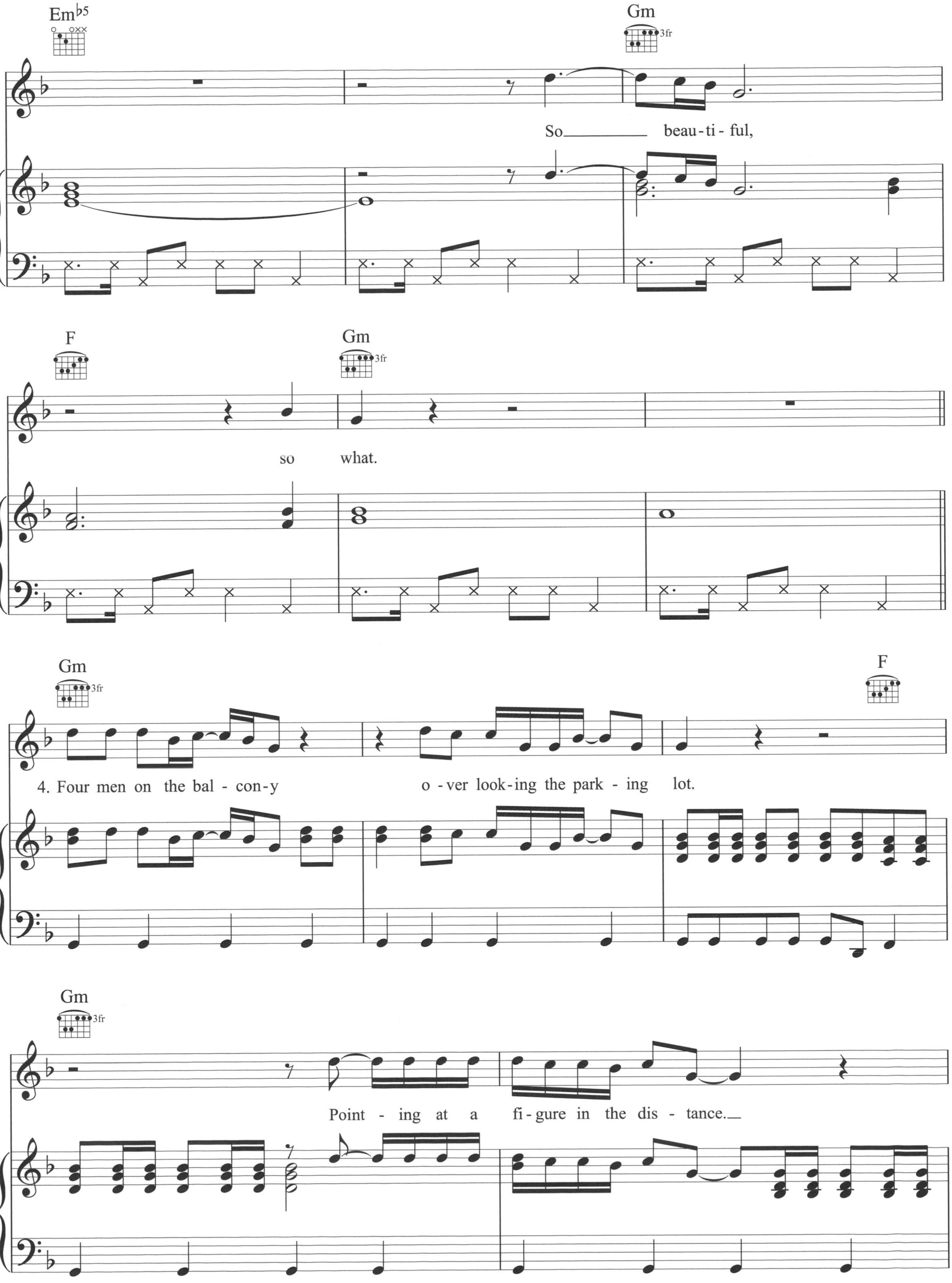
Em♭5
Gm
So beau-ti-ful,
F
Gm
so what.
Gm
F
4. Four men on the bal-con-y o-ver look-ing the park-ing lot.
Gm
Point-ing at a fi-gure in the dis-tance.

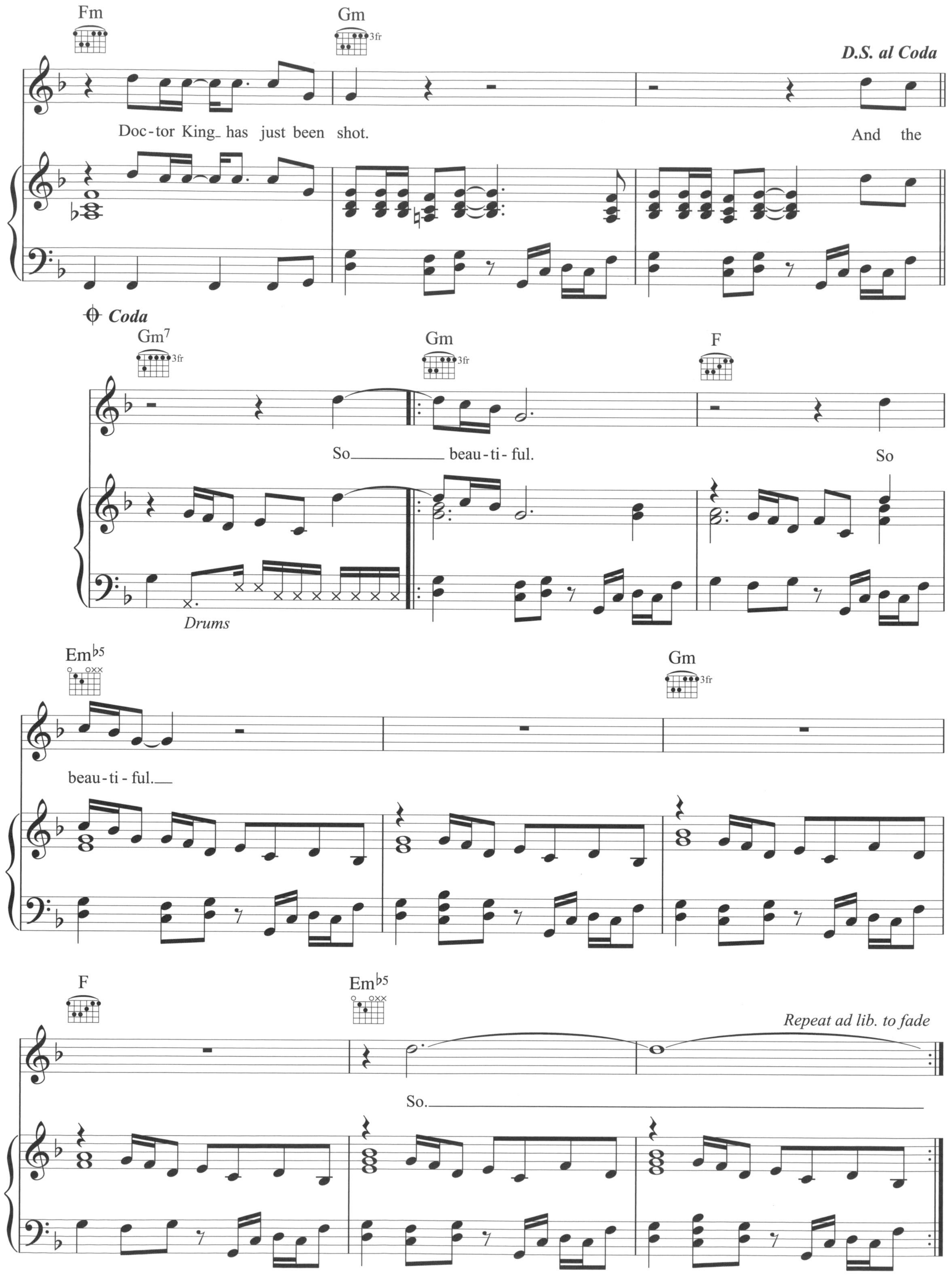
Fm
Gm
3fr
D.S. al Coda
Doc-tor King_ has just been shot.
And the
Coda
Gm7
3fr
Gm
3fr
F
So_______ beau-ti-ful.
So
Drums
Em♭5
Gm
3fr
beau-ti-ful.__
F
Em♭5
Repeat ad lib. to fade
So.____________________

1 2 3 4 5 6 7 8 9